Working With
The
Mental Health Act 1983

Written by

Steven Richards *BA (Hons)* & Aasya F Mughal *LLB (Hons), Barrister*

www.matrixtrainingassociates.com

First published in September 2006 by

Matrix Training Associates
2 The Green
North Waltham
Hampshire RG25 2BQ

www.matrixtrainingassociates.com

British Library Cataloguing in Publication Data
A catalogue record for this book is available from the British Library

ISBN 978-0-9552349-1-0

Printed and bound in England

Working With The Mental Health Act 1983

CONTENTS

Working With The Mental Health Act 1983

INTRODUCTION

The Mental Health Act 1983 provides the authority and means to detain and treat people with a mental disorder in hospital. It also allows for the supervision of people in the community. It is a substantial and sometimes complex piece of legislation. The Act is arranged like a book and is divided into chapters called Parts. Each Part contains numbered paragraphs called sections. The expression that a person has been 'sectioned' actually means that they are subject to the powers of a numbered paragraph of the legislation. In all there are 149 separate sections, each relating to different powers and rules governing the operation of the legislation.

The sections of the Act that specifically provide the power to detain a person vary in several ways including:

- their duration – from 6 hours to many years
- the professionals involved – nurse, doctor, police officer, social worker
- treatment – whether a person can be given treatment without their consent
- discharge – who can discharge the person
- appeals – the person's right of appeal against detention

Facts

On any one day there are, on average, 14,700 people detained across England and Wales[1]. Figures for 2005 show that as a percentage of all patients on mental health wards, 46% of men and 29% of women were detained under the Act[2].

Current issues relating to the Act

Amending the Act

Government plans for a new Mental Health Act were abandoned in March 2006 after seven years of consultation[3]. This means that the current Mental Health Act 1983 will remain in place for many more years. At the time of writing (September 2006), the government has announced proposals to amend some parts of the 1983 legislation. However, it will take several years before these come into effect and the planned amendments will leave the vast majority of the 1983 Act unchanged. The proposed amendments are discussed on page 97.

The Mental Capacity Act 2005

The Mental Capacity Act comes into force in April 2007 and will overlap with the Mental Health Act 1983 in a number of areas. Services will face a choice between the two Acts when dealing with the care and treatment of people with mental disorder whose capacity is called into question. The interaction between the two Acts is explored on page 103.

Discrimination

Concern over discrimination within mental health services and in the use of the current Act has resulted in a regular census of patients in mental health hospitals in England and Wales. In 2005 the census found that people whose ethnic origin was *Black Caribbean, Black African* or *Black Other* were 33-44% more likely to be detained compared to the average for all patients. They were also more likely to be placed in seclusion and 29% more likely to be subject to control and restraint[2]. The government is attempting to address this issue through the five year action plan *Delivering Race Equality in Mental Health Care*[4].

Powers

The powers of the Mental Health Act are considerable as they override two basic rights. Normally, a person can only be detained if they have committed an offence. Under the legislation however, a person is detained not because of any crime but because they have a mental disorder that needs hospital treatment. The other basic right is that if an adult has capacity, they can only be given treatment with their consent. Again, the Act overrides this and so makes psychiatry unique in the medical profession for permitting such action against an adult who has capacity.

Protection

Staff who detain a person and give them treatment against their will are afforded the protection of the legislation if they apply the Act correctly.

Duties

The powers of the Act and the protection given to staff are only accessible by following the legislation. Staff have a duty to follow the requirements of the Act if they wish to make use of its powers.

Rights

People who are detained under the Act are given legal rights, the most prominent of which is the right of appeal to the Mental Health Review Tribunal (and also to the Hospital Managers). The Tribunal is an independent judicial body that has the power to discharge detained patients. In addition, the Mental Health Act Commission has a separate independent role to monitor the general use of the legislation and the care of people detained under it.

Limitations

Whilst the powers of the Act are considerable, the legislation is limited in its application. To be detained a person has to meet certain criteria, all of which act to reduce the number of people affected by the legislation. The Act is largely confined to in-patient settings and treatment can only be given for mental disorder. Being placed on a section does not mean staff can take control of finances or make any other treatment decisions without consent.

Age range of the Act

The Act does not have a lower or upper age limit. However, for those aged 17 and younger the legislation overlaps with the Children Act 1989 and in such cases services should choose which is the most appropriate legislation (see page 109).

Where is the Act effective?

The Act is effective in, and its powers limited to, England and Wales.

Note

This guide provides a detailed explanation of the Mental Health Act 1983, however it should not be regarded as a substitute for the Act itself. Nothing in it is intended to be, or should be, relied upon as legal advice. If you have any comments on the content or suggestions for future editions email: *books@matrixtrainingassociates.com*.

The guide follows the format of the Act and uses the masculine form (he/his) throughout. Similarly, the term 'patient' is also used in accordance with the legislation.

- **Definition of mental disorder** – the Act is limited in use to people who have a mental disorder. The legislation provides guidance on the definition of the disorders it includes and also those it excludes.

- **Powers to admit and treat people in hospital** – over 20 different sections provide the power to detain a person for assessment and/or treatment of a mental disorder. Each section differs in relation to a number of matters including the time period involved, the professionals required, the appeal procedures and the treatment regulations.

- **Nearest relative** – an important part of the Act that formally assigns a nearest relative to a detained person and gives that relative authority within the legislation.

- **Criminal and Court related powers** – a series of sections that allows Courts and prisons to transfer people from the criminal justice system to hospital for assessment and treatment of mental disorder.

- **Treatment** – the power to override a detained person's wishes and give them treatment for mental disorder without their consent. The legislation provides a number of mechanisms to safeguard this power and limits its use to certain treatments.

- **Mental Health Review Tribunal** – the independent judicial body to which many detained patients can appeal. A Tribunal consists of three members who meet the patient and the clinical team treating them. It has the power to discharge the patient from section at the end of the hearing.

- **Hospital Managers** – under the Act the Hospital Managers represent the NHS Trust (or other body) that formally detains a person. They have a number of duties under the legislation including holding appeal hearings for patients. They have the power to discharge patients from a section following the hearing.

- **Mental Health Act Commission** – the official body created by the Act that monitors the use of the legislation and makes regular visits to review the care and treatment of detained patients. The Commission also provides guidance and information on the legislation.

- **Code of Practice** – a statutory code concerning the practical use of the Act. It is updated periodically and represents current thinking on best practice when using the legislation.

- **Criminal offence** – a criminal offence which can be used to prosecute any individual responsible for the care of someone who appears to have a mental disorder, if they ill-treat or neglect that person.

- **Protection for staff** – under Section 139 staff are protected from civil or criminal proceedings for the actions they take when using the legislative powers to physically detain and forcibly treat people. This protection is only available if the Act has been used properly and does not apply if the actions in question were done in bad faith or without reasonable care.

- **Private hospitals** – non NHS units such as independent private hospitals or care homes can use the Act but they must be registered to do so and special safeguards within the Act apply to them, for example measures to address financial conflicts of interest.

Working With The Mental Health Act 1983

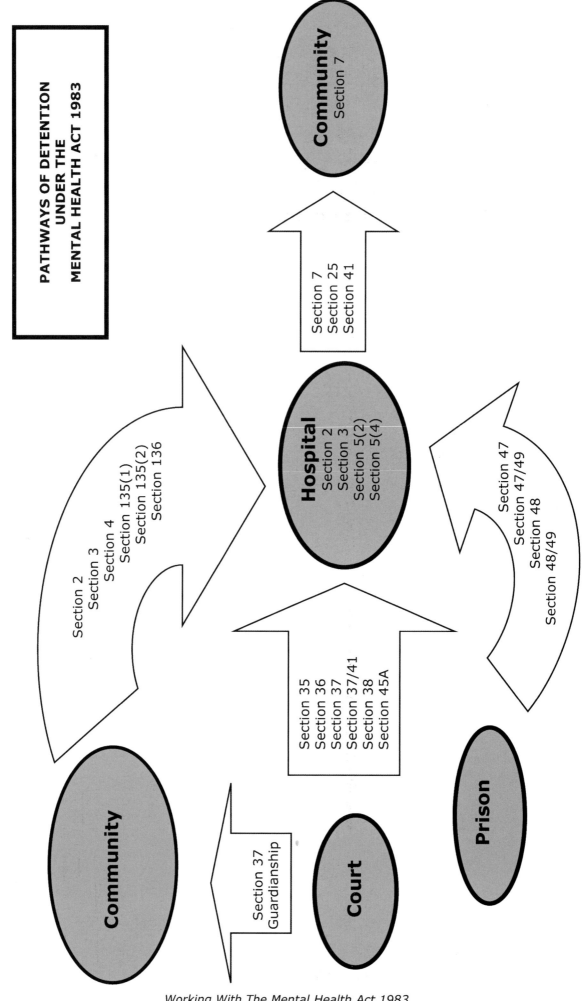

Community
Section 7

Section 7
Section 25
Section 41

Hospital
Section 2
Section 3
Section 5(2)
Section 5(4)

Section 2
Section 3
Section 4
Section 135(1)
Section 135(2)
Section 136

Section 47
Section 47/49
Section 48
Section 48/49

Section 35
Section 36
Section 37
Section 37/41
Section 38
Section 45A

Section 37
Guardianship

Community

Court

Prison

Working With The Mental Health Act 1983

The Act provides powers to admit people who are living in the community to hospital by force. This becomes necessary when a professional believes a person needs to be admitted to hospital and the person concerned does not wish to go on a voluntary basis. Six different sections can be used and they differ in a number of ways. Sections 2 and 3 require the involvement of three professionals and provide the power to detain a person for at least a month. Section 4 is a short-term emergency power. Sections 135(1) and 135(2) provide specific powers to enter locked premises and require a magistrate's authorisation. Finally, there is Section 136 which is the only section under the Act that the police have sole jurisdiction over.

Section	Professionals required	Duration
Section 2	Two doctors and an approved social worker or nearest relative	up to 28 days
Section 3	Two doctors and an approved social worker or nearest relative	up to 6 months
Section 4	A doctor and a social worker or nearest relative	up to 72 hours
Section 135(1)	A magistrate, a police officer, an approved social worker and a doctor	up to 72 hours
Section 135(2)	A magistrate and a police officer	up to 72 hours
Section 136	A police officer	up to 72 hours

Summary The power to detain and treat a person in hospital for up to 28 days. It is used for the assessment of people who have, or are believed to have a mental disorder.

The section can be used in a number of ways; to bring a person from the community into hospital, to prevent a voluntary in-patient leaving hospital or to detain a patient for a longer period if they are already on a short-term section, for example Section 4, 5(2), 135(1) or 136.

Legal criteria

The person is suffering from mental disorder

↓

and it is of a *nature or degree* to warrant detention in hospital for assessment (or assessment followed by treatment) for at least a limited period

↓

and the person ought to be detained in the interests of their own health **or** safety **or** with a view to the protection of others.

Powers

- *Detention* – the power to detain a person for up to 28 days in hospital.

- *Treatment* – the person can be given treatment for mental disorder with or without their consent (see page 64).

- *Absconding* – if the person absconds they can be forcibly returned to hospital by any authorised member of hospital staff or by the police.

Who is involved? Two doctors – one of whom must be Section 12 approved (have experience of psychiatry) and both doctors should not work at the same hospital site (however, they could work for the same NHS Trust). In addition, if practicable, one doctor should already know the person
and
an approved social worker or the nearest relative (known as 'the applicant').

Each person can make separate recommendations for the section or they can make a joint assessment. Each must interview the patient and at least one doctor must discuss the case with the applicant.

The statutory forms require the doctors to give reasons why informal (voluntary) admission is not appropriate. The approved social worker must state that detention under Section 2 is the most appropriate way of providing the care and treatment the person needs. If neither doctor knew the person before making their recommendations the social worker (or nearest relative) must explain why it was not possible to use a doctor who knew the person.

Time limits *Medical forms* – there must be no more than five days between the two medical examinations. *Application* – the applicant (approved social worker or nearest relative) must have seen the person in the 14 days prior to making the application. *Admission* – the person must be admitted to hospital within 14 days from the date of the last medical interview for the section.

Leave of absence	The consultant (RMO) can grant leave of absence (Section 17) for any period of time. However, since Section 2 is a short-term assessment power, prolonged leave would not be considered good practice.
Patient rights	The right of appeal to the Mental Health Review Tribunal within 14 days of the section commencing. The right of appeal to the Hospital Managers at any time. The right to be visited by and complain to the Mental Health Act Commission.
Duties on staff	Staff should take all practicable steps to ensure the patient understands their legal rights and provide this information both orally and in writing (*Patient Rights Leaflet 6*). If an approved social worker completes the section they are obliged, before or within a reasonable time after, to take such steps as are practicable to inform the person's nearest relative that a Section 2 is to be, or has been made and inform the relative of their legal rights.
Discharge	There are a number of ways for the section to end: ❖ Discharge by the consultant (RMO) before the end of the 28 days ❖ Discharge by a Mental Health Review Tribunal ❖ Discharge by a Hospital Managers' hearing ❖ Discharge by the nearest relative ❖ Lapse of the Section 2 after the 28 days. Allowing the section to expire through passage of time would not be considered good practice as any detention should end as soon as the legal criteria are no longer met.
Extending the section	Although Section 2 cannot itself be extended, a person can be detained for a further period of time by the completion of a Section 3 before the Section 2 expires.
Forms	Form 1 or 2 - application by nearest relative or approved social worker Form 3 or 4 - joint or single medical recommendations Form 14 - acceptance of section papers Form 15 - receipt of medical recommendations
Code of Practice	Section 2 may be considered appropriate when the diagnosis and prognosis are unclear, or assessment is needed to formulate a treatment plan, or a person is already known to mental health services but their condition has changed and needs re-assessment, or a person has not had a previous admission to hospital and has not been in regular contact with mental health services.
Facts	In 2004-05 Section 2 was used 22,500 times, making it the second most used detention power after Section 3[1].
Amending the Act	Section 2 will be partially affected by the planned changes to the definition of mental disorder and the additional professionals who can undertake the roles of responsible medical officer and approved social worker.

Working With The Mental Health Act 1983

SECTION 3
ADMISSION FOR TREATMENT

Summary This section gives the power to detain and treat a person in hospital for up to six months. The power can be extended (renewed) for further periods of time if required.

The section can be used in a number of ways; to bring a person from the community into hospital, to prevent a voluntary in-patient leaving hospital or to detain a patient for a longer period of time if they are already on a short-term section, for example Section 2, 4, 5(2), 135(1) or 136.

Legal criteria

The person is suffering from mental illness, severe mental impairment, psychopathic disorder or mental impairment

↓

and it is of a *nature or degree* which makes it appropriate for them to receive treatment in a hospital
(in the case of psychopathic disorder or mental impairment - treatment is likely to alleviate or prevent a deterioration of their condition)

↓

and it is necessary for the health **or** safety of the person **or** for the protection of others that they receive treatment

↓

and treatment cannot be provided unless they are detained.

Powers
- *Detention* – the power to detain a person for up to 6 months initially.

- *Treatment* – the person can be given treatment for mental disorder with or without their consent (see page 64).

- *Absconding* – if the person absconds they can be forcibly returned to hospital by any authorised member of hospital staff or by the police.

Who is involved? Two doctors – one of whom must be Section 12 approved (have experience of psychiatry) and both doctors should not work at the same hospital site (however, they could work for the same NHS Trust). In addition, if practicable, one doctor should already know the person
and
an approved social worker or the nearest relative (known as 'the applicant').

Each person can make separate recommendations for the section or they can make a joint assessment. Each must interview the patient and at least one doctor must discuss the case with the applicant. If neither doctor knew the person before making their recommendations, the nearest relative or social worker must explain why. The social worker must state that detention in hospital is the most appropriate way of providing the care and treatment the person needs.

The doctors must give reasons why the stated mental disorder is of a nature or degree that makes it appropriate for treatment in hospital, and in addition why treatment can only be provided under detention. They should state why other options such as a home treatment team, assertive outreach or informal (voluntary) admission are not appropriate.

Working With The Mental Health Act 1983

Time limits	*Medical forms* – there must be no more than five days between the two medical examinations. *Application* – the applicant (approved social worker or nearest relative) must have seen the person in the 14 days prior to making the application. *Admission* – the person must be admitted to hospital within 14 days from the date of the last medical interview for the Section 3.
Leave of absence	The consultant (RMO) may grant leave of absence (Section 17) for any period of time.
Patient rights	The right of appeal to the Mental Health Review Tribunal once during each period of detention. The right of appeal to the Hospital Managers at any time. The right to be visited by and complain to the Mental Health Act Commission.
Duties on staff	Staff should take all practicable steps to ensure the patient understands their legal rights and provide this information both orally and in writing (*Patient Rights Leaflet 7*). The approved social worker must consult the patient's nearest relative (unless such consultation is not reasonably practicable or would involve unreasonable delay) as part of their assessment. If the relative objects to the section, it cannot proceed. A section can then only be completed if the relative is displaced or removed by a Court. If the person does not appeal to the Mental Health Review Tribunal in the first six months and the section is then extended, the hospital must refer their case to the Tribunal. If the person has not had a Tribunal hearing for three years, again their case must be referred to the Tribunal. Note: if the person is under 16, the period is reduced to one year for referral. The provision of after-care services under Section 117 upon discharge.
Discharge	There are a number of ways for the section to end: ❖ Discharge by the consultant (RMO) before the end of the six months ❖ Discharge by a Mental Health Review Tribunal ❖ Discharge by a Hospital Managers' hearing ❖ Discharge by the nearest relative ❖ Lapse of the section at the end of the detaining period. Allowing the section to expire through passage of time would not be considered good practice as any detention should end as soon as the legal criteria are no longer met. ❖ Transfer to Section 25 supervised discharge in the community
Extending the section	The section can be extended (renewed) before it ends by the consultant (RMO) for a further six month period and thereafter yearly. The consultant must examine the patient and consult with at least one other person who is professionally involved in their treatment before completing the renewal using Form 30.

Court rulings on renewals have stated that it is lawful to renew a Section 3 whilst the patient is on leave provided they are receiving, or are expected to receive, hospital treatment (the definition of which includes out-patient appointments and/or ward rounds) and that this makes up a significant element of their care plan.

The legal criteria for renewal are:

The person is suffering from mental illness, severe mental impairment, psychopathic disorder or mental impairment

and the mental disorder is of a *nature or degree* which makes it appropriate for them to receive medical treatment in a hospital

and such treatment is likely to alleviate or prevent a deterioration of their condition (alternatively in the case of mental illness or severe mental impairment - if the person is discharged they are unlikely to be able to care for themselves, to obtain the care they need, or to guard themselves against serious exploitation)

and it is necessary for the health **or** safety of the person **or** for the protection of others that they should receive such treatment
and it cannot be provided unless they continue to be detained.

Forms	Form 8 or 9 - application by nearest relative or approved social worker Form 10 or 11 - joint or single medical recommendations Form 14 - acceptance of section papers Form 15 - receipt of medical recommendations When completing the Section 3 the two doctors making the recommendations must agree on at least one form of mental disorder on their forms.
Code of Practice	Factors that indicate a Section 3 would be appropriate include when a person's mental disorder is already known to the team and they have been assessed in the recent past or when a person is already on Section 2 and treatment will be required beyond the 28 days of that section.
Case Law	A person can be detained if their mental illness is either of a *nature or degree* to warrant detention. Both requirements do not have to be satisfied. In the case of R (details below) the patient's drug and alcohol abuse were part of the *nature* of his mental illness and had to be addressed in deciding whether the statutory criteria for continued detention were met. The criterion of *degree* did not also have to be satisfied. *(From the case of: R (on the application of the Home Secretary) v MHRT and (1) DH, (2) South West London & St George's Mental Health NHS Trust. [2003] EWHC 2864, November 2003)*
Facts	Section 3 is the most used detention power of the Act. For the year ending March 2005, it was used a total of 23,000 times[1].
Amending the Act	Section 3 will be partially affected by the planned changes to the definition of mental disorder, the abolition of the treatability test and the additional professionals who can undertake the roles of responsible medical officer and approved social worker.

Working With The Mental Health Act 1983

SECTION 4
ADMISSION FOR ASSESSMENT IN CASES OF EMERGENCY

Summary
A section that allows a person to be admitted from the community and detained in hospital for up to 72 hours. It may be applied when staff want to place a person under Section 2 (28 days) but are unable to get two doctors as required and the person needs to be admitted urgently.

Legal criteria

It is of urgent necessity for the person to be admitted and detained under Section 2 of the Act (see the legal criteria for Section 2 on page 7)

and compliance with the requirements of Section 2 (two doctors and a social worker) would involve undesirable delay.

Powers

- *Admission and detention* – the power to admit someone forcibly from the community to hospital and detain them for up to 72 hours.

- *Treatment* – the person can only be given treatment for mental disorder with their consent.

- *Absconding* – if the person absconds they can be forcibly returned to hospital by any authorised member of hospital staff or by the police.

Who is involved?
One doctor – if practicable they should already know the person
and
an approved social worker or the nearest relative (known as the 'applicant').

The doctor must state that an emergency exists and give the number of hours delay it would cause to get a second doctor (to complete Section 2 instead) and that such delay might result in harm to the patient or those caring for them or other persons.

If the doctor did not know the person before making their recommendation, the social worker or nearest relative must explain why it was not possible to use a doctor who knew the person. The social worker must state that detention in hospital is the most appropriate way of providing the care and treatment the person needs.

Time limits
Application – at the time of making the application, the social worker or nearest relative must have seen the person during the previous 24 hours.

Admission – the person must be admitted to hospital within 24 hours of either the doctor's examination or the social worker's or nearest relative's application being made – whichever is earliest.

Detention – the 72 hour period of detention begins with the admission of the person to hospital.

Leave of absence
Does not apply as Section 4 is a short-term section for assessment.

Patient rights	There is no right of appeal to the Mental Health Review Tribunal or the Hospital Managers. The right to be visited by and complain to the Mental Health Act Commission.
Duties on staff	Staff should take all practicable steps to ensure the patient understands their legal rights and provide this information both orally and in writing (*Patient Rights Leaflet 2*).
Discharge	There are two ways for the section to end: ❖ If the assessment for Section 2 or 3 that takes place during the 72 hour period concludes that neither is required, the consultant (RMO) should discharge the section. ❖ The section expires after 72 hours. Allowing the section to expire through passage of time would not be considered good practice as the assessment for Section 2 or 3 should take place within the 72 hour period.
Extending the section	*Section 2* – the Section 4 can be 'converted' to a Section 2 within the 72 hours with the addition of a second medical recommendation. *Section 3* – if a Section 3 is completed within the 72 hours it overrides the Section 4. The medical recommendation used in the original Section 4 cannot be used as one of the medical recommendations for the Section 3.
Forms	Form 5 or 6 - application by nearest relative or approved social worker Form 7 - medical recommendation Form 14 - acceptance of section papers Form 15 - receipt of medical recommendation
Code of Practice	The Code states that Section 4 should not be used because it is more convenient for the second doctor to see the person in hospital. Section 4 is designed for use in an emergency so there must be evidence of immediate and significant risk of mental or physical harm to the person, to others or to property.
Practical advice	When converting to a Section 2 from a Section 4, the two medical forms when taken together, must comply with the requirements of Section 2. That is, at least one must be from a Section 12 approved doctor and both doctors should not work at the same hospital. The converted Section 2 will run from the date the person is admitted to hospital. A social worker (or nearest relative) does not have to be involved but they should be informed that the section has been converted.
Facts	In 2004-05 there were 1,300 admissions to hospital using Section 4. This was a reduction of 20% from the previous year[1].
Amending the Act	Section 4 will be partially affected by the planned changes to the definition of mental disorder and the additional professionals who can undertake the role of an approved social worker.

Summary   The power to forcibly enter a property to look for and remove a person to a place of safety (usually hospital) for assessment for a period of up to 72 hours.

Legal criteria

It appears to a magistrate that there is reasonable cause to suspect that a person believed to be suffering from mental disorder

has been, or is being, ill-treated, neglected or kept otherwise than under proper control
or
is living alone and unable to care for themselves.

Powers

- *Entry* – the power to forcibly enter locked premises, on one occasion only, to look for a person.

- *Removal* – the power to remove the person, if considered necessary, to a place of safety (usually hospital).

- *Detention* – the power to detain the person for up to 72 hours with a view to completing a Section 2 or 3.

- *Treatment* – the person can only be given treatment for mental disorder with their consent.

- *Absconding* – if the person absconds they can be forcibly returned to hospital by any authorised member of hospital staff or by the police.

Who is involved?

An approved social worker – who makes the application to a magistrate
and
a magistrate – who issues the Section 135(1) warrant
and
a police officer – who is authorised by the section to enter locked premises by force and remove the person. The police officer must be accompanied by an approved social worker and a doctor.

Time limits

Warrant – the warrant must be used within one month of being issued.

Detention – the 72 hour period of detention begins from the person's admission to hospital.

Leave of absence   Does not apply as this is a short-term section for assessment.

Patient rights   There is no right of appeal to the Mental Health Review Tribunal or the Hospital Managers.

The right to be visited by and complain to the Mental Health Act Commission.

Duties on staff	Staff should take all practicable steps to ensure the patient understands their legal rights and provide this information both orally and in writing (*Patient Rights Leaflet 4*).
Discharge	There are two ways for the section to end:
	❖ Those making the assessment for Section 2 or 3 may decide that neither is appropriate.
	❖ The section expires after the 72 hours. Allowing the section to expire through passage of time would not be considered good practice as the assessment for Section 2 or 3 should take place within the 72 hour period.
Extending the section	Although Section 135(1) only lasts for 72 hours, a person can be detained further by the completion of a Section 2 or 3 before the Section 135(1) ends.
Forms	The magistrate will issue a Section 135(1) warrant.
Practical advice	If the name of the person is unknown, the warrant can be made out by the Court to an unnamed individual.
Facts	For the year ending March 2005, Sections 135(1) and 135(2) were used 314 times[1].
Amending the Act	Section 135(1) will be partially affected by the planned changes to the definition of mental disorder and the additional professionals who can undertake the role of the approved social worker.

SECTION 135(2)
WARRANT TO SEARCH FOR AND REMOVE A PATIENT

Summary   The power to forcibly enter a property to look for and remove a detained patient who has absconded from hospital. If the person allows entry to the property voluntarily there is no need to obtain a Section 135(2).

Legal criteria

On information given, it appears to a magistrate that

there is reasonable cause to believe that a patient already under section is to be found on premises within the jurisdiction of the magistrate

and admission to the premises has already been refused or a refusal of such admission is predicted.

Powers

- *Entry* – the power to forcibly enter locked premises, on one occasion only, to look for a person.

- *Removal* – the power to remove the person if found on the premises.

- *Detention* – once found the person returns to the conditions of the original section under which they were detained.

Who is involved?   An authorised person (for example from the NHS Trust) or a police officer – who makes the application to a magistrate
and
a magistrate – who issues the Section 135(2) warrant
and
a police officer – who is authorised by the section to enter locked premises by force and remove the person. The police officer may or may not be accompanied by a doctor or other authorised person.

Time limits   The warrant must be executed (used) within one month of being issued.

Leave of absence   Does not apply as this is a short term section.

Patient rights   There is no right of appeal to the Mental Health Review Tribunal or the Hospital Managers.

The right to be visited by and complain to the Mental Health Act Commission.

Duties on staff   There is no rights leaflet for this section as it is used to return a person, who is already on a section, to the place they were detained. Those using Section 135(2) should inform the person of the power they are using to enter the premises, however the rights that apply are those of the section the person was under at the time they absconded from hospital.

Working With The Mental Health Act 1983

17

Discharge	The section ends once the premises are entered and the person is removed. At this point the person comes under the powers of the section they were under at the time they absconded.
Extending the section	Does not apply.
Forms	The magistrate will issue a Section 135(2) warrant.
Amending the Act	Section 135(2) will not be affected by the planned amendments to the Act.

SECTION 136
POLICE POWER OF ARREST

Summary A section that allows a police officer to take a person they have found in a public place, who appears in need of care or control, to a place of safety for assessment for up to 72 hours.

Legal criteria

A police officer finds, in a place to which the public have access, a person who appears to be suffering from mental disorder

↓

and the person appears to be in immediate need of care or control

↓

and the police officer considers it necessary in the interests of that person **or** for the protection of other persons, to remove them to a place of safety.

Powers

- *Detention* – the person can be detained for up to 72 hours in a place of safety (usually hospital or a police station).

- *Treatment* – the person can only be given treatment for mental disorder with their consent.

- *Absconding* – if the person absconds they can be forcibly returned to hospital by any authorised member of hospital staff or by the police.

Who is involved? One police officer.

Time limits The 72 hour period of detention begins when the person arrives at the place of safety.

Leave of absence Does not apply as this is a short-term section for assessment.

Patient rights There is no right of appeal to the Mental Health Review Tribunal or the Hospital Managers.

The right to be visited by and complain to the Mental Health Act Commission.

Duties on staff The Code of Practice recommends that assessment should begin as soon as possible once the person arrives at the place of safety.

Staff should take all practicable steps to ensure the patient understands their legal rights and provide this information both orally and in writing (*Patient Rights Leaflet 5*).

Discharge The section requires that the person is assessed by both a doctor (where possible Section 12 approved) and an approved social worker within the 72 hours. If, following assessment, they do not feel that a Section 2 or 3 is appropriate, the Section 136 will end.

Working With The Mental Health Act 1983

Extending the section	Although Section 136 only lasts for 72 hours, a person can be detained further by the completion of a Section 2 or 3 before the Section 136 ends.
Forms	The police officer will complete a police form for Section 136.
Code of Practice	*Place of safety* The preferred place of safety is hospital, however each area must decide on the most appropriate places of safety available to them and their use in different circumstances. *Assessment by an approved social worker* An approved social worker must always be called to assess a person under Section 136. However, if the doctor making the assessment does so before the social worker arrives and decides the person does not have a mental disorder under the Act, the person should be released from the Section 136 immediately.
Case Law	Private land, even if adjacent to a public place, does not come within the meaning of a 'public place' under Section 136. In this case, a private garden with very little space between it and a public place could not be interpreted as a public place even if harm could be inflicted on passers-by from that garden. *(From the case of: R v Leroy Lloyd Roberts [2003] EWCA Crim 2753, October 2003)*
Facts	For the year ending March 2005, 4,753 people were brought to hospital under Section 136. After assessment, 28% were placed on Section 2 or 3 and the remainder were either admitted informally or discharged[1].
Amending the Act	Section 136 will not be affected by the planned amendments to the Act.

If hospital staff feel that the powers of the Act are required, the following sections may be used. They provide authority to detain a voluntary (informal) in-patient who refuses treatment and/or wishes to leave hospital. Under the Act, a hospital is any NHS in-patient unit, either mental health or general. In addition, appropriately registered private hospitals and care homes are also considered to be hospitals in this context. It should be noted however that private hospitals and care homes have special rules that apply to them in order to safeguard against financial conflicts of interest.

The hospital sections are:

Section	Professionals required	Duration
Section 2 *	Two doctors and an approved social worker or the nearest relative	up to 28 days
Section 3 *	Two doctors and an approved social worker or the nearest relative	up to 6 months
Section 5(2)	One doctor	up to 72 hours
Section 5(4)	One nurse	up to 6 hours

Sections 2 and 3 are the most commonly used detention powers of the Act and can be used both in hospital, to prevent a person leaving, and in the community to bring a person into hospital and detain them there.

Sections 5(2) and 5(4) are short-term emergency powers that are designed to prevent a voluntary in-patient discharging themselves. The duration of the sections allows time for the longer term powers of Section 2 or Section 3 to be applied.

* Note: Full details on Section 2 and Section 3 are given in the previous chapter *Community to Hospital* (pages 7 to 11).

SECTION 5(2)
APPLICATION IN RESPECT OF A PATIENT ALREADY IN HOSPITAL

Summary
A section that allows for the detention of a person already in hospital for up to 72 hours. It is designed to provide the time required to complete a Section 2 or 3 when the person wishes to leave hospital before the necessary arrangements for these sections can be made.

Legal criteria

The person is a voluntary in-patient in hospital

and it appears to the doctor that an application
ought to be made for a Section 2 or 3.

Powers
- *Detention* – the power to detain a person who is already in hospital for up to 72 hours.

- *Treatment* – the person can only be given treatment for mental disorder with their consent.

- *Absconding* – if the person absconds they can be forcibly returned to hospital by any authorised member of hospital staff or by the police.

Who is involved?
One doctor – the doctor in charge of the person's treatment or their nominated deputy. Hospitals should have a policy in place for the appointment of nominated deputies in the absence of the consultant. (See *Code of Practice* within this section).

The doctor must give reasons why informal (voluntary) treatment is no longer appropriate.

Time limits
There are no specific time limits except the 72 hour period of the section itself.

Leave of absence
Does not apply as this is a short-term section.

Patient rights
There is no right of appeal to the Mental Health Review Tribunal or the Hospital Managers.

The right to be visited by and complain to the Mental Health Act Commission.

Duties on staff
Staff should take all practicable steps to ensure the patient understands their legal rights and provide this information both orally and in writing (*Patient Rights Leaflet 3*).

Discharge
There are a number of ways for the section to end:

❖ It is decided that an assessment for further detention under Section 2 or 3 is not required.

❖ The assessment for a Section 2 or 3 concludes that neither is required.

❖ The section expires after the 72 hour period. Allowing the section to expire through passage of time would not be considered good practice as the assessment for Section 2 or 3 should take place within the 72 hour period.

Working With The Mental Health Act 1983

Extending the section	Although Section 5(2) only lasts up to 72 hours a person can be detained further by the completion of a Section 2 or 3 before the Section 5(2) ends.
Forms	Form 12 – medical recommendation Form 14 – acceptance of section papers Form 15 – receipt of medical recommendation
Code of Practice	*Personal examination* Section 5(2) should only be used after the patient has been personally examined by a doctor. A doctor should not complete a Section 5(2) form and leave it on a ward (without the date or time on it) to be used in case the patient wishes to leave at some point in the future. *Consultants* If the doctor completing the section is not a consultant they should, wherever possible, speak to a consultant before using the power. *Out of hours* It is common practice, out of hours, for the junior on-call doctor at a hospital to be assigned the role of nominated deputy for the consultants at the site. In this role they can use Section 5(2). *Transfer* Patients under Section 5(2) should not be transferred to another hospital. The Mental Health Act Commission has produced a guidance note on transferring detained patients (see page 123).
Facts	Section 5(2) was used 8,232 times for the year ending March 2005 following which 42% of people were not placed on a further section[1].
Amending the Act	Section 5(2) will not be affected by the planned amendments to the Act.

SECTION 5(4)
NURSES POWER

Summary   The power for a nurse to detain a voluntary in-patient for up to six hours. The person has to indicate they wish to leave hospital and there has to be an immediate need to prevent this where a doctor is not available to complete a Section 5(2) instead.

The section is intended as an emergency measure when a doctor is not immediately available and it ends with the arrival of a doctor on the ward.

Legal criteria

A person is receiving treatment for mental disorder as an in-patient in hospital

and the disorder is of such a degree that it is necessary for their
health **or** safety **or** for the protection of others
for them to be immediately restrained from leaving hospital

and it is not practicable to secure the immediate attendance of a
doctor to complete a Section 5(2) instead.

Powers
- *Detention* – the power to detain a patient for up to six hours.

- *Treatment* – the person can only be given treatment for mental disorder with their consent.

- *Absconding* – if the person absconds they can be forcibly returned to hospital by any authorised member of hospital staff or by the police.

Who is involved?   One nurse. They must be qualified to the Nursing and Midwifery Council level of registered nurse:

    (i)   Level 1 mental health
    (ii)   Level 2 mental health
    (iii)   Level 1 learning disability
    (iv)   Level 2 learning disability

Time limits   There are no specific time limits except the six hour duration of the section itself.

Leave of absence   Does not apply as this is a short-term emergency section.

Patient rights   There is no right of appeal to the Mental Health Review Tribunal or the Hospital Managers.

The right to be visited by and complain to the Mental Health Act Commission.

Duties on staff   Staff should take all practicable steps to ensure the patient understands their legal rights and provide this information both orally and in writing (*Patient Rights Leaflet 1*).

Working With The Mental Health Act 1983

25

Discharge	Section 5(4) is discharged when a doctor arrives within the six hour period. It is not considered good practice for the section to run the full six hours and then expire without a doctor arriving.
Extending the section	When the doctor arrives a Section 5(2) can be applied instead. If this is the case, the six hour period of the Section 5(4) is included within the 72 hour period of the Section 5(2).
Forms	Form 13 – Nursing recommendation starting the section Form 16 – Nursing report ending the section (arrival of doctor)
Code of Practice	Section 5(4) is designed for use in emergency situations and any doctor with the power to use Section 5(2) instead should ensure that they arrive on the ward as soon as possible to undertake a medical assessment. A nurse cannot be directed by others to use this power. Whether the legal criteria are met and the use of the power is appropriate is a matter for the professional judgment of the individual nurse concerned. The use of Section 5(4) should be closely monitored by hospital management.
Facts	Section 5(4) was used 1,839 times during the year ending March 2005[1].
Amending the Act	Section 5(4) will not be affected by the proposed amendments to the Act.

The powers and nature of the two community sections are very similar. However, while social services are primarily responsible for guardianship, the NHS is the lead service for supervised discharge. In addition, supervised discharge contains greater authority to make a person attend necessary appointments.

Guardianship was part of the original 1983 Act, whereas supervised discharge was added to the legislation over a decade later under the Mental Health (Patients in the Community) Act 1995, in response to a number of high profile cases which indicated problems with discharge in the community.

Section	Name	Duration
Section 7	Guardianship	up to 6 months initially
Section 25	Supervised Discharge	up to 6 months initially

Community sections have been one of the most contentious areas of the Act, specifically the debate over whether they contain the power to forcibly treat a person in the community. To date this has not been the case. However, the government is proposing to introduce a new community based section called a *supervised community treatment order* when it amends the Act. Whether this proposed amendment makes it through the parliamentary process is yet to be seen. See page 97 for further details.

Summary A community based section that lasts for up to six months and may be extended (renewed) for further periods of time. Although guardianship has few enforceable powers, in practice many people comply with the requirements of the order. It can be used both as an alternative to admitting people to hospital and as a route to discharge people from hospital.

Legal criteria

A person who is aged at least 16 years is suffering from mental illness, severe mental impairment, psychopathic disorder or mental impairment

↓

and it is of a *nature or degree* to warrant the need for guardianship

↓

and it is necessary in the interests of the welfare of the person **or** for the protection of others that guardianship is used.

Powers

- *Residence* – the power to require the person to live at a place specified by the guardian. If the person absconds from that place, they can be forcibly returned. However, this does not mean the person can be forced to move to a specific place or be detained there.

- *Appointments* – the power to require the person to attend appointments for treatment, occupation, education or training. This does not mean the person can be forced to attend appointments.

- *Access* – the power to require the person to see a doctor, approved social worker or other staff member at the person's place of residence. This does not mean the power to force entry to the person's residence to see them.

- *Treatment* – the person can only be given treatment with their consent.

Who is involved?

Two doctors – one of whom must be Section 12 approved (have experience of psychiatry) and both doctors should not work at the same hospital site (they could work for the same NHS Trust). If practicable, one doctor should already know the person
and
an approved social worker or the nearest relative (known as 'the applicant').

The applicant must state who the guardian will be, either a local authority (social services) or a named person. If the guardian is not a local authority, the proposed guardian must state in writing that they are willing to act as guardian and that the local authority have accepted this.

The approved social worker is required to consult the person's nearest relative (unless such consultation is not reasonably practicable or would involve unreasonable delay) as part of their assessment. If the relative objects to the section, it cannot proceed. A section can then only be completed if the relative is displaced by a Court.

Time limits	There should be no more than five days between the medical examinations. The applicant (approved social worker or nearest relative) must have seen the person in the 14 days prior to making their application. The guardianship forms must be received by the local authority within 14 days of the second doctor's examination.
Leave of absence	Does not apply as the person is living in the community.
Patient rights	The right of appeal to the Mental Health Review Tribunal once during each period of detention.
	The right of appeal to the local authority (social services).
	The right to be visited by and complain to the Mental Health Act Commission.
Duties on staff	Staff should take all practicable steps to ensure the patient understands their legal rights and provide this information both orally and in writing (*Patient Rights Leaflet 10*).
	The responsible local authority must arrange for a doctor (Section 12 approved) to visit the person at least once a year.
Discharge	There are a number of ways for the section to end:
	❖ Discharge by the doctor responsible for the guardianship (this may be a consultant, general practitioner or other doctor)
	❖ Discharge by the responsible local authority (social services)
	❖ Discharge by a Mental Health Review Tribunal
	❖ Discharge by the nearest relative
	❖ Lapse of the section at the end of the detaining period. Allowing the section to expire through passage of time would not be considered good practice as any detention should end as soon as the legal criteria are no longer met.
	❖ The use of Section 3 (if the person is admitted to hospital). However, where a person under guardianship is in hospital voluntarily or under Section 2, 4, 5(2) or 5(4) the guardianship order does not end but its powers are suspended until the person is discharged into the community (unless the time period of the guardianship order has expired in the meantime).
	❖ Transfer to hospital under Section 19 of the Act. The transfer requires two medical recommendations plus social services approval and acts in such a way that on admission the guardianship is converted into a Section 3.
Extending the section	If a further period of detention is needed, the section can be extended (renewed) for a further six months and thereafter yearly. Only the consultant (RMO) can renew the section and this is done by completing Form 31. The doctor must examine the person and consult with at least one other person who has been professionally involved with the person's treatment. The completed form has to be presented to the guardian and, if they are different, the local authority. Unless the guardian or local authority discharges the guardianship order, the renewal will take effect.

The legal criteria for renewal is:

The person is suffering from mental illness, severe mental impairment, psychopathic disorder or mental impairment

and the disorder is of a *nature or degree* which warrants their reception into guardianship

and it is necessary in the interests of the person's welfare **or** for the protection of others that the person should remain under guardianship.

Forms	Form 15	- receipt of medical recommendation
	Form 17 or 18	- application by nearest relative or approved social worker
	Form 19 or 20	- joint or single medical recommendations
	Form 21	- record of acceptance of guardianship application

The two doctors making recommendations must agree on at least one form of mental disorder on their forms.

Code of Practice The production of a comprehensive care plan should always be part of the process of applying for guardianship.

Practical advice *Admission to hospital (Section 116)*
If the person is admitted to hospital there is a legal obligation on the guardian, if they are a local authority, to arrange regular visits to see the person.

Change of guardian (Section 10 (1)(2))
If the guardian dies or writes to the local authority to say they no longer wish to be guardian the power transfers to the local authority. In addition, if the guardian becomes incapacitated for any reason their functions may, during the period of incapacity, be performed by the local authority or someone approved by the local authority.

Guardian not appropriate (Section 10(3))
If the guardian is not performing their functions properly, an approved social worker can apply to the County Court to have the guardian removed.

People involved in Court proceedings (Section 22)
There are special provisions in the Act for people subject to guardianship who are detained in custody by the Courts.

Facts For the year ending 31 March 2005, there were 466 new guardianship sections completed including guardianships made by the Courts. At the end of March 2005 there were 966 people on guardianship sections[5].

Amending the Act Guardianship will be partially affected by the planned changes to the definition of mental disorder and the additional professionals who can undertake the roles of responsible medical officer and approved social worker.

Working With The Mental Health Act 1983

SECTION 25
SUPERVISED DISCHARGE

Summary A community based section that runs for up to six months and can be extended (renewed) for further periods of time. It is similar to guardianship but is centred on the NHS rather than the local authority (social services).

Legal criteria

A person aged 16 or over is detained under Section 3, 37, 47 or 48

and they are suffering from mental illness, severe mental impairment, psychopathic disorder or mental impairment

and there would be a *substantial* risk of *serious* harm to the health **or** safety of the person **or** the safety of others
or that the person will be seriously exploited
if they do not receive the after-care services to be provided for them after they leave hospital

and being subject to supervised discharge is likely to help ensure that they receive the after-care services they require.

Powers The section provides four requirements that can placed upon the person. The NHS Trust and local authority have the discretion to use any combination of the four requirements.

- *Residence* – the power to require the person to live at a specified place. Failure to comply provides authority for the person to be taken to this place. However, this does not include the power to detain the person at their residence.

- *Appointments* – the power to require the person to attend appointments for occupation, education and training. Failure to comply provides authority for the person to be taken to the appointment by force. This does not include the power to detain the person at the place of appointment once there.

- *Access* – the power to require the person to provide access to their place of residence to their supervisor, a doctor, an approved social worker or to any other person authorised by the supervisor.

- *Treatment* – the power to require the person to attend appointments for treatment. Failure to comply provides authority for the person to be taken to the appointment by force. However, there is no power to forcibly treat the person without their consent.

Failure to comply with the requirements of the supervised discharge triggers a review of the section which can change the after-care provided and/or the requirements of the section, lead to an assessment for admission to hospital (Section 3) or end the supervised discharge.

Who is involved?	The consultant (RMO) – who makes an application (see *Duties on staff*) **and** a doctor who, if possible, will be involved with the patient after they leave hospital, makes a second recommendation. If the consultant (RMO) making the application is also the doctor who will be involved with the patient following discharge (the community responsible medical officer – CRMO) the second recommendation can be made by any doctor **and** an approved social worker.

In addition, once the section is completed, the community consultant (CRMO) and community supervisor (often an approved social worker or community psychiatric nurse) must formally agree to their respective roles. Details of the after-care must also be provided (Care Programme Approach documents). |
| **Time limits** | Supervised discharge can only be completed whilst the person is detained under Section 3, 37, 47 or 48 (they could be in hospital or on leave). However, its powers only come into force when they are discharged from one of these sections and hospital. |
| **Leave of absence** | Does not apply as the person is in the community. |
| **Patient rights** | The right of appeal to the Mental Health Review Tribunal once during each period of detention. The nearest relative has the same right.

The right to be visited by and complain to the Mental Health Act Commission. |
| **Duties on staff** | Staff should take all practicable steps to ensure the patient understands their legal rights and provide this information both orally and in writing (*Patient Rights Leaflet 17*).

• *Consulting*
Before making an application for supervised discharge, renewing it or discharging it, the consultant (CRMO) is responsible for ensuring the following people are consulted and their views taken into account:

the patient, at least one professional involved in the medical treatment, at least one professional involved in the after-care, the supervisor, a carer (if any) and the nearest relative (but only if practicable to do so).

Before modifying the after-care arrangements or the requirements of the supervised discharge, the following people must be consulted and their views taken into account:

the patient, the carer (if any) and the nearest relative.

• *Informing*
When an application for supervised discharge is made, or an application is accepted, or is renewed, or ends (discharged), or the consultant (CRMO) is changed, or the supervisor is changed, or the conditions of the order are modified or the after-care is modified the following people must be informed:

the patient (orally and in writing), the carer (if there is one) and the nearest relative (in writing).

In addition, when an application is made and then accepted any people consulted before the application was made must be informed. |

Note: at any point when the nearest relative is to be consulted or informed the patient may request that they are not. This request must be followed unless the patient has a propensity to violent or dangerous behaviour towards others and the consultant considers it appropriate to contact the relative.

The section should be reviewed if the person refuses or neglects to receive after-care services or to comply with the requirements of the section.

Discharge	There are a number of ways for the section to end: ❖ Discharge by the consultant (CRMO) using Form 6S ❖ The person is admitted to hospital and detained under Section 3 or 37 ❖ The person is placed under a Section 7 guardianship order ❖ Discharge by a Mental Health Review Tribunal ❖ Lapse of the section at the end of the detaining period. Allowing the section to expire through passage of time would not be considered good practice as any detention should end as soon as the legal criteria are no longer met.
Extending the section	The section can be extended (renewed) by the consultant for a further six month period and thereafter yearly. The community consultant (CRMO) must examine the person and confirm they meet the requirements laid out in the *Legal criteria* category for supervised discharge (other than being under Section 3) using Form 5S (see *Duties on staff*).
Forms	Form 1S – application for supervised discharge Form 2S – medical recommendation Form 3S – approved social worker's recommendation The two medical recommendations must agree on at least one form of mental disorder.
Practical advice	If the person is admitted to hospital as a voluntary (informal) patient or put on Section 2, 4, 135, 136 or detained in custody (including remand) by a Court, the supervised discharge is suspended for a period of time (Section 25I). For more information see the *Memorandum to the Act* available at *www.markwalton.net*.
Facts	The use of supervised discharge has grown slowly from 562 cases in the year 2000 to 643 cases for the year ending March 2005[1].
Amending the Act	It is not clear if the planned introduction of a new community section called supervised community treatment will replace supervised discharge, amend it or become an alternative to it. If supervised discharged remains unchanged it will be partially affected by the planned changes to the definition of mental disorder and the additional professionals who can undertake the roles of responsible medical officer and approved social worker.

FORENSIC (COURT AND PRISON) SECTIONS

Sections that relate to Court and criminal proceedings are contained in Part III of the Act. Part III is one of the most complex parts of the legislation due to the number of sections and the individual rules that apply to each one. The different detention sections relate to the various stages in the criminal justice process (see the diagram below). In addition, because of the nature of some offences, restrictions are applied which lead to the involvement of the Home Office (see *Forensic Restricted Sections*, page 53). Figures show that Court and prison sections account for 6% of all sections and in 2004-05 they were used a total of 1,664 times[1].

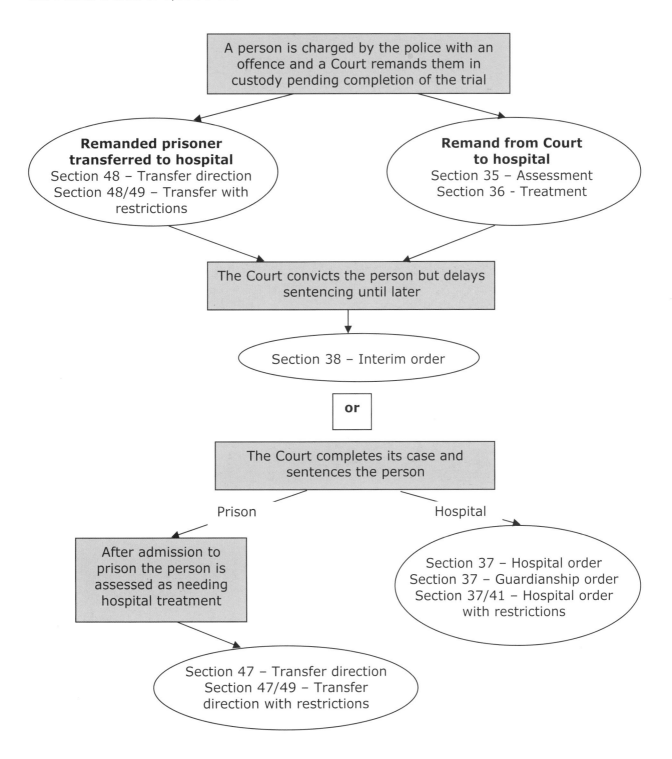

Working With The Mental Health Act 1983

SECTION 35
REMAND TO HOSPITAL FOR ASSESSMENT

Summary   A person on remand may be sent by a Court to hospital for assessment for up to 28 days, which can be extended up to a maximum 12 weeks. The hospital is required to provide the Court with a report on the person as to the extent of any mental disorder.

Legal criteria

Crown Court: the person is awaiting trial for an offence punishable by imprisonment, or has been arraigned for such an offence but has not yet been sentenced or otherwise dealt with for the offence

or

Magistrates' Court: the person has been convicted of an offence punishable on summary conviction with imprisonment, or is charged with an offence punishable with imprisonment and either the Court is satisfied that they did the act or made the omission charged or that the person has consented to the use of Section 35

and the Court is satisfied on the written or oral evidence of a doctor that there is reason to suspect the person is suffering from mental illness, severe mental impairment, psychopathic disorder or mental impairment

and it would be impracticable for a report on their mental condition to be completed if they were remanded on bail.

Powers

- *Detention* – the power to detain the person for up to 28 days initially.

- *Treatment* – the person can only be given treatment for mental disorder with their consent.

- *Absconding* – if the person absconds they can be arrested (without a warrant) by a police officer and taken to Court. The Court may choose to end the section and continue with the original criminal proceedings.

Who is involved?   A Magistrates' Court or Crown Court – makes the order
and
a doctor who is Section 12 approved (has experience of psychiatry) – who gives written or oral evidence to the Court.

Time limits   The Court must be satisfied that the person will be admitted to hospital within seven days of the order being made.

Leave of absence   There is no provision in the Act for leave to be granted to patients on this section.

Patient rights   The right to obtain, at their own expense, an independent psychiatric report and use this to apply to the Court for the section to be discharged.

There is no right of appeal to the Mental Health Review Tribunal or the Hospital Managers.

The right to be visited by and complain to the Mental Health Act Commission.

Working With The Mental Health Act 1983

Duties on staff	Staff should take all practicable steps to ensure the patient understands their legal rights and provide this information both orally and in writing (*Patient Rights Leaflet 14*).
Discharge	There are a number of ways for the section to end: ❖ The Court may discharge the section at any time it appears appropriate to do so or when the Court case is concluded and sentence passed. ❖ The Court is presented with an independent medical report initiated by the patient which states they do not have a mental disorder. ❖ The hospital reports that the person does not need further assessment.
Extending the section	If more time is needed to complete the assessment, the Court can extend the section for further periods of 28 days, up to a maximum of 12 weeks. To extend the section a doctor must give written or oral evidence to the Court. The person does not have to attend the hearing but their legal representative must. The Court can extend the person's detention at the end of the criminal process by sentencing them to hospital under Section 37.
Forms	The Court issues a Section 35 remand order.
Code of Practice	The Court is responsible for transporting the person to hospital after making the order. However, once admitted to hospital, the hospital is responsible for returning the person to Court for future hearings and also for providing an escort for the person when travelling to Court from hospital. Once the person is at Court, they come under the supervision of the police or prison officers there.
Practical advice	This section is not covered by the treatment powers of the Act so medication can only be given if the person consents. However, if the person refuses treatment and the consultant feels that it is needed, they can refer back to the Court with a recommendation for either a Section 36 (but only a Crown Court can make this order) or a Section 37. If the Court cannot provide a hearing and treatment is assessed as being urgent, it is possible to complete a Section 2 or 3 whilst a person is also subject to Section 35 so that the person is effectively detained under two sections. This enables the person to be given treatment without their consent under the powers of Section 2 or 3. This is a controversial use of the Act and was not envisaged when the legislation was written, however the Code of Practice does agree to such practice.
Facts	Section 35 was used by the Courts 118 times for the year ending March 2005[1].
Amending the Act	Section 35 will be partially affected by the planned changes to the definition of mental disorder and the additional professionals who can undertake the role of responsible medical officer.

SECTION 36
REMAND TO HOSPITAL FOR TREATMENT

Summary   A person on remand is sent by the Crown Court to hospital for treatment lasting up to 28 days. The section can be extended for up to 12 weeks in total.

Legal criteria

Crown Court: A person charged with an offence punishable with imprisonment, is either in custody awaiting trial or awaiting sentence, following trial

and they are suffering from mental illness or severe mental impairment of a *nature or degree* which makes it appropriate for them to be detained in hospital for treatment.

Powers

• *Detention* – the power to detain the person for up to 28 days initially.

• *Treatment* – the person can be given treatment for mental disorder with or without their consent (see page 64).

• *Absconding* – if the person absconds they can be arrested (without a warrant) by a police officer and taken to Court. The Court may choose to end the section and continue with the original criminal proceedings.

Who is involved?   Two doctors – one of whom must be Section 12 approved (have experience of psychiatry). The doctors can submit written reports to the Court or attend in person to give an oral report. Both doctors can be from the same NHS Trust **and**
a Crown Court (a Magistrates' Court cannot make this order).

Time limits   The person must be admitted to hospital within seven days of the order being made.

Leave of absence   There is no provision in the Act for leave to be granted to patients on this section.

Patient rights   The right to obtain, at their own expense, an independent psychiatric report and use this to apply to the Court for the section to be discharged.

There is no right of appeal to the Mental Health Review Tribunal or the Hospital Managers.

The right to be visited by and complain to the Mental Health Act Commission.

Duties on staff   Staff should take all practicable steps to ensure the patient understands their legal rights and provide this information both orally and in writing (*Patient Rights Leaflet 15*).

Discharge	There are a number of ways for the section to end:
	❖ The Court may discharge the section at any time it appears appropriate to do so or when the Court case is concluded and sentence passed.
	❖ The Court is presented with an independent medical report initiated by the patient which states they do not have a mental disorder.
	❖ The hospital reports that the person does not need treatment.
Extending the section	The section can be extended for further periods of 28 days up to a total of 12 weeks. To do this the consultant (RMO) provides a written report to the Court, or attends in person and requests a further period of time. The Court will decide whether to extend the section or not. The person does not have to attend the hearing but their legal representative must.
	The Court can continue hospital detention at the end of the criminal justice process by sentencing the person to hospital under Section 37.
Forms	The Crown Court issues a Section 36 remand order.
Code of Practice	The Court is responsible for organising the transportation of the person to hospital after making the order. However, once admitted to hospital, the hospital is responsible for returning the person to Court for future hearings and also for providing an escort for the person when travelling to Court from hospital. Once the person is at Court, they come under the supervision of the police or prison officers there.
Facts	Section 36 is rarely used and for the year ending March 2005 there were only 12 recorded cases[1].
Amending the Act	Section 36 will be partially affected by the planned changes to the definition of mental disorder and the additional professionals who can undertake the role of responsible medical officer.

Summary   A Court may order (sentence) a person to hospital for treatment for up to six months, which can be extended for further periods of time. Section 37 operates like a Section 3 once the person is admitted to hospital. A Section 37 may also be made with a restriction order from the Home Office attached. It is then known as Section 37/41 (see page 55).

Legal criteria

Magistrates' Court: a person is convicted of an offence punishable on summary conviction with imprisonment or
Crown Court: a person is convicted of an offence punishable with imprisonment

and the person is suffering from mental illness, severe mental impairment, psychopathic disorder or mental impairment

and the mental disorder is of a *nature or degree* which makes it appropriate for them to be detained in hospital for treatment
(for psychopathic disorder or mental impairment, such treatment is likely to alleviate or prevent a deterioration of their condition)

and the Court is of the opinion that the most suitable method of dealing with the person is by means of this section.

Powers   • *Detention* – the power to detain the person for up to six months initially.

   • *Treatment* – the person can be given treatment for mental disorder with or without their consent (see page 64).

   • *Absconding* – if the person absconds they can be forcibly returned to hospital by any authorised member of hospital staff or by the police.

Who is involved?   Two doctors – one of whom must be Section 12 approved (have experience of psychiatry). The doctors can provide written recommendations or give oral evidence before the Court. The doctors can work for the same NHS Trust. The medical forms must agree on at least one form of mental disorder
and
a Crown Court or Magistrates' Court – which makes the order.

Time limits   The person must be admitted to hospital within 28 days of the order being made. If they are not admitted immediately, they can be detained for up to 28 days in a place of safety (for example prison) whilst a hospital bed is arranged.

Leave of absence   The consultant (RMO) can grant leave of absence (Section 17) for any period of time.

Working With The Mental Health Act 1983

Patient rights	The right of appeal to the Mental Health Review Tribunal, but only in the second six months and then once in each subsequent period of detention. The patient's nearest relative has the same right.
	The right of appeal to the Hospital Managers at any time.
	The right to be visited by and complain to the Mental Health Act Commission.
	The right to appeal to the Crown Court or Court of Appeal to have the conviction quashed or a different sentence imposed.
Duties on staff	Staff should take all practicable steps to ensure the patient understands their legal rights and provide this information both orally and in writing (*Patient Rights Leaflet 12*).
	If the patient has not had a Mental Health Review Tribunal hearing for three years, the hospital must refer their case to the Tribunal.
	The provision of after-care services under Section 117 upon discharge.
Discharge	There are a number of ways for the section to end:
	❖ Discharge by the consultant (RMO)
	❖ Discharge by a Mental Health Review Tribunal
	❖ Discharge by a Hospital Managers' hearing
	❖ Discharge by the Crown Court or Court of Appeal (this may result in the person being sentenced again but under criminal law)
	❖ Transfer to Section 25 (supervised discharge) or Section 7 (guardianship) into the community
	❖ Lapse of the section at the end of the detaining period. Allowing the section to expire through passage of time would not be considered good practice as any detention should end as soon as the legal criteria are no longer met.
Extending the section	The section can be extended (renewed) before it ends by the consultant (RMO) for a further six month period and thereafter yearly. The renewal criteria and process are the same as for Section 3 (see page 9).
Forms	The Court issues a Section 37 hospital order.
Code of Practice	The Court is responsible for transporting the person to hospital after making the order.
Practical advice	With Section 37 the Court passes responsibility for the person over to the hospital. Once in hospital, the Court has no further input and theoretically the consultant (RMO) could discharge the section immediately.
	A person's mental state at the time of the offence is not part of the consideration for applying Section 37.
Facts	Section 37 is the most used forensic section. For the year ending March 2005 there were 349 admissions to hospital from Section 37 Court orders[1].
Amending the Act	Section 37 will be partially affected by the planned changes to the definition of mental disorder, the abolition of the treatability test and the additional professionals who can undertake the role of responsible medical officer.

Working With The Mental Health Act 1983

Summary
A Court may order (sentence) a person to guardianship in the community for up to six months, which may be extended for further periods of time. It operates like a Section 7 guardianship order.

Legal criteria

Magistrates' Court: a person is convicted of an offence punishable on summary conviction with imprisonment or
Crown Court: a person is convicted of an offence punishable with imprisonment

and the person is suffering from mental illness, severe mental impairment, psychopathic disorder or mental impairment

and the person has reached the age of 16 and the mental disorder is of a *nature or degree* which warrants their reception into guardianship

and the Court is of the opinion that the most suitable method of dealing with the case is by means of this section.

Powers
- *Residence* – the power to require the person to live at a place specified by the guardian. If the person absconds from this place, they can be forcibly returned. However, this does not mean the person can be forced to move to a specified place or be detained there.

- *Appointments* – the power to require the person to attend appointments for treatment, occupation, education or training. However, this does not mean the person can be forced to attend appointments.

- *Access* – the power to require the person to see any doctor, approved social worker or other member of staff at the person's place of residence. However, this does not mean the power to force entry to the person's residence.

- *Treatment* – the person can only be given treatment with their consent.

Who is involved?
Two doctors – one of whom must be Section 12 approved (have experience of psychiatry). The doctors can provide written recommendations or give oral evidence before the Court. The doctors can work for the same NHS Trust. They must both agree on at least one form of mental disorder
and
a Crown Court or Magistrates' Court – which makes the order.

The Court will name a local authority (social services) or a person approved by the local authority to act as guardian.

Time limits
No time limits apply.

Leave of absence	Does not apply as the person is in the community.
Patient rights	The right of appeal to the Mental Health Review Tribunal once during each period of detention. The nearest relative also has an independent right of appeal to the Tribunal but only once in the first year and then once in every subsequent year. The right of appeal to the local authority (social services). The right to be visited by and complain to the Mental Health Act Commission. The right of appeal to the Crown Court or Court of Appeal to have the conviction quashed or a different sentence imposed.
Duties on staff	Staff should take all practicable steps to ensure the patient understands their legal rights and provide this information both orally and in writing (*Patient Rights Leaflet 11*). If the person has not had a Mental Health Review Tribunal hearing for three years, the local authority must refer their case to the Tribunal.
Discharge	There are a number of ways for the section to end: ❖ Discharge by the consultant (RMO) ❖ Discharge by a Mental Health Review Tribunal ❖ Discharge by the local authority ❖ Discharge by the Crown Court or Court of Appeal (this may result in the person being sentenced again but under criminal law) ❖ Lapse of the section at the end of the detaining period. Allowing the section to expire through passage of time would not be considered good practice as any detention should end as soon as the legal criteria are no longer met.
Extending the section	The section can be extended (renewed) before it ends by the consultant (RMO) for a further six month period and thereafter yearly.
Forms	The Court issues a Section 37 guardianship order.
Practical advice	With Section 37 the Court places the person into guardianship. Once under guardianship, the Court has no further input or responsibility.
Amending the Act	Section 37 will be partially affected by the planned changes to the definition of mental disorder and the additional professionals who can undertake the role of responsible medical officer.

Summary   A Court order that allows a hospital to detain a convicted offender, initially for up to 12 weeks, in order to assess whether a full hospital order (Section 37) is appropriate. The section can be extended for up to a maximum of one year.

Legal criteria

A person convicted by a Crown Court or Magistrates' Court
of an offence punishable with imprisonment

and the person is suffering from mental illness, severe mental impairment,
psychopathic disorder or mental impairment

and there is reason to suppose that the mental disorder from which
the person is suffering is such that it may be appropriate
for a hospital order (Section 37) to be made.

Powers
- *Detention* – the power to detain the person for up to 12 weeks initially.

- *Treatment* – the person can be given treatment for mental disorder with or without their consent (see page 64).

- *Absconding* – if the person absconds they can be arrested (without a warrant) by a police officer and then taken to Court. The Court may choose to end the section and deal with the person in another way.

Who is involved?   Two doctors – one of whom must be Section 12 approved (have experience of psychiatry). One doctor must be from the NHS Trust that will treat the person and both doctors may work for the same NHS Trust. The doctors can provide written medical recommendations or give oral evidence before the Court.
and
a Crown Court or Magistrates' Court – which makes the order.

Time limits   The person must be admitted to hospital within 28 days of the order being made.

Leave of absence   There is no provision in the Act to grant leave for patients under this section.

Patient rights   The right of appeal to the Crown Court or Court of Appeal to have the conviction quashed or a different sentence imposed.

There is no right of appeal to the Mental Health Review Tribunal or the Hospital Managers.

The right to be visited by and complain to the Mental Health Act Commission.

Duties on staff   Staff should take all practicable steps to ensure the patient understands their legal rights and provide this information both orally and in writing (*Patient Rights Leaflet 16*).

Working With The Mental Health Act 1983

Discharge	There are a number of ways for the section to end:
	❖ Discharge by the Crown Court or Court of Appeal (this may result in the person being sentenced again but under criminal law)
	❖ Following the hospital's assessment, the Court will decide whether to convert the section into a Section 37 (thereby ending the Court's involvement) or deal with the person in some other way.
Extending the section	The section initially lasts for up to 12 weeks and can then be extended by the Court for further periods of up to 28 days for a maximum of one year.
	Extensions are made on the written or oral evidence of the consultant (RMO) to the Court. The person does not have to attend Court but they must have a legal representative at the hearing.
Forms	The Crown Court or Magistrates' Court issues a Section 38 order.
Code of Practice	The Court is responsible for organising the transportation of the person to hospital after making the order. However, once admitted to hospital, the hospital is responsible for returning the person to Court for future hearings and for providing an escort for the person when travelling from hospital to Court. Once the person is at Court, they come under the supervision of the police or prison officers there.
Amending the Act	Section 38 will be partially affected by the planned changes to the definition of mental disorder and the additional professionals who can undertake the role of responsible medical officer.

Summary The transfer of a sentenced prisoner to hospital and their detention there for up to six months initially. Once in hospital, the section operates like a Section 37 hospital order. A Section 47 is usually made with a restriction order from the Home Office attached. It is then known as Section 47/49 (see page 59).

Legal criteria

The person is serving a sentence of imprisonment

↓

and the Secretary of State is satisfied they are suffering from mental illness, severe mental impairment, psychopathic disorder or mental impairment

↓

and the mental disorder is of a *nature or degree* which makes it appropriate for them to be detained in hospital for treatment
(for psychopathic disorder or mental impairment, the treatment is likely to alleviate or prevent a deterioration of their condition)

↓

and the Secretary of State, having regard to the public interest and all the circumstances may direct that the person is removed to and detained in hospital.

Powers
- *Detention* – the power to detain the person for up to six months initially.

- *Treatment* – the person can be given treatment for mental disorder with or without their consent (see page 64).

- *Absconding* – if the person absconds they can be forcibly returned to hospital by any authorised member of hospital staff or by the police.

Who is involved? Two doctors – one of whom must be Section 12 approved (have experience of psychiatry). Both doctors can work for the same NHS Trust.
and
the Home Office – which agrees and issues the transfer direction.

It is important to note that the Home Office is not obliged to agree to a Section 47 despite two medical recommendations being made. It will consider whether the prisoner can be safely contained by the hospital taking into account a number of risk factors including the nature of the offence, the length of the sentence and the risk of absconding.

Time limits The person must be admitted to hospital within 14 days of the Section 47 order being made.

Leave of absence The consultant (RMO) can grant leave of absence (Section 17) for any period of time.

Patient rights	The right of appeal to the Mental Health Review Tribunal in the first six months and then once in each subsequent period of detention.

The right of appeal to the Hospital Managers at any time.

The right to be visited by and complain to the Mental Health Act Commission. |
| **Duties on staff** | Staff should take all practicable steps to ensure the patient understands their legal rights and provide this information both orally and in writing (*Patient Rights Leaflet 19 + Home Office letter addressed to the person*).

The provision of after-care services under Section 117 upon discharge.

If the person has not had a Mental Health Review Tribunal hearing for three years, the hospital must refer their case to the Tribunal. |
| **Discharge** | There are a number of ways for the section to end:

❖ Discharge by the consultant (RMO)

❖ Discharge by a Mental Health Review Tribunal

❖ Discharge by a Hospital Managers' hearing |
| **Extending the section** | The section can be extended (renewed) before it ends by the consultant (RMO) for a further six month period and yearly thereafter. |
| **Forms** | The Home Office issues a Section 47 transfer direction.

The two doctors making recommendations must agree on at least one form of mental disorder on their forms. |
Code of Practice	Upon transfer the prison or remand centre should send the hospital a current medical report together with a report from the prison healthcare staff on the person's general care and also any relevant pre-sentence reports from the probation service.
Practical advice	A Section 47 without a restriction order operates like a Section 37 (hospital order) when the person is admitted to hospital.
Amending the Act	Section 47 will be partially affected by the planned changes to the definition of mental disorder, the abolition of the treatability test and the additional professionals who can undertake the role of responsible medical officer.

SECTION 48
REMOVAL TO HOSPITAL OF UNSENTENCED PRISONERS

Summary

The transfer of an unsentenced prisoner to hospital and their detention there. In the majority of cases a Section 48 is made with a restriction order from the Home Office attached. It is then known as Section 48/49 (see page 61).

Legal criteria

An unsentenced prisoner who is either detained in prison or a remand centre, or remanded in custody by a Magistrates' Court, or committed to prison by a Court for a limited term, or detained under the Immigration Act 1971 (or Section 62 of the Nationality, Immigration and Asylum Act 2002)

and the Secretary of State is satisfied that the person is suffering from mental illness or severe mental impairment of a *nature or degree* which makes it appropriate for them to be detained and treated in hospital

and the person is in urgent need of such treatment.

Powers

- *Detention* – the power to detain the person until the Court process is concluded.

- *Treatment* – the person can be given treatment for mental disorder with or without their consent (see page 64).

- *Absconding* – if the person absconds they can be forcibly returned to hospital by any authorised member of hospital staff or by the police.

Who is involved?

Two doctors – one of whom must be Section 12 approved (have experience of psychiatry). Both doctors may be from the same NHS Trust.
and
the Home Office – which agrees and issues the transfer direction.

It is important to note that the Home Office is not obliged to agree to a Section 48 despite two medical recommendations being made. It will consider whether the prisoner can be safely contained by the hospital taking into account a number of risk factors including the nature of the offence, their behaviour in prison and the risk of absconding.

Time limits

The person must be admitted to hospital within 14 days of the Section 48 being made by the Secretary of State.

Leave of absence

The consultant (RMO) can grant leave of absence (Section 17) for any period of time.

Patient rights

The right of appeal to the Mental Health Review Tribunal once in the first six months and then once in each subsequent period of detention.

The right of appeal to the Hospital Managers at any time.

The right to be visited by and complain to the Mental Health Act Commission.

Working With The Mental Health Act 1983

Duties on staff	Staff should take all practicable steps to ensure the patient understands their legal rights and provide this information both orally and in writing (*Patient Rights Leaflet 20 + Home Office letter addressed to the person*). The provision of after-care services under Section 117 upon discharge.
Discharge	There are a number of ways for the section to end: ❖ The consultant (RMO) may inform the Home Office or Court that the person no longer requires treatment in hospital or that no effective treatment can be provided for them. ❖ Discharge by a Mental Health Review Tribunal ❖ Discharge by a Hospital Managers' hearing In all of the above cases, the Home Office and Court must be informed as they may issue an order for the person to be returned to prison or for immigration detainees, returned to detention. ❖ The Court case to which the person is subject ends and they are sentenced.
Extending the section	Section 48 remains in place until the Court or Home Office direct its conclusion.
Forms	The Home Office issues a Section 48 transfer direction.
Code of Practice	Upon transfer the prison or remand centre should send the hospital a current medical report together with a report from the prison healthcare staff on the person's general care and also any relevant pre-sentence reports from the probation service.
Facts	There were just 20 people transferred under Section 48 orders for the year ending March 2005. This compares with 346 people transferred via Section 48/49 orders during the same period[1].
Amending the Act	Section 48 will be partially affected by the planned changes to the definition of mental disorder and the additional professionals who can undertake the role of responsible medical officer.

FORENSIC RESTRICTED SECTIONS

Restricted sections are applied when it is thought that a person requires extra supervision for the protection of the public at large. The order is either made at the point of sentencing by a Court or through the transfer of a prisoner to hospital by the Secretary of State for the Home Office. The restriction means that decisions concerning leave, transfer and discharge must involve the Home Office. Under the Act restricted sections are the responsibility of the Secretary of State, however in practice a department of the Home Office undertakes the legal requirements on behalf of the Minister.

Contact

Mental Health Unit
The Home Office, 2nd Floor, Fry Building, 2 Marsham Street, London SW1P 4DF.

Tel: 020 7035 1484   Fax: 020 7035 8974   Website: www.homeoffice.gov.uk

Guidance

The Mental Health Unit at the Home Office has produced the following guidance notes for staff working with restricted patients. These can be downloaded from the website listed above.

- Notes for the Guidance of Social Supervisors Mental Health Act 1983 Supervision and Aftercare of Conditionally Discharged Restricted Patients (April 2006)

- Notes for the Guidance of Supervising Psychiatrists Mental Health Act 1983 Supervision and Aftercare of Conditionally Discharged Restricted Patients (April 2006)

- Guidance for Responsible Medical Officers: Leave of Absence for Patients Subject to Restrictions (March 2005)

- Procedure for the Transfer of Prisoners to and from Hospital under Sections 47 and 48 of the Mental Health Act 1983 (November 2005)

Facts

During the year ending December 2004, there were 1,329 restricted sections made, the greatest number being transfers from prison (Sections 47/49 and 48/49) which totalled 831[6].

At any one time the number of people on restricted sections in hospital (Sections 37/41, 47/49, 48/49) is approximately 3,200[6]. The high security hospitals (Broadmoor, Ashworth and Rampton) accommodate a third of this population[7].

Note

Section 45A (hospital direction with limitation direction), which was added to the Act via the Crime (Sentences) Act 1997, is not detailed in the following pages. This is because it was not used during the 12 month period ending March 2005 and was used only twice the previous year[1]. Section 45A is a Court sentence to hospital for someone with psychopathic disorder. At any time after admission, if the consultant (RMO) feels that treatment is no longer required or beneficial, the person can be transferred back to prison to serve the remainder of their sentence. On admission to hospital it operates like a Section 47/49 which is detailed on page 59.

SECTION 37/41
HOSPITAL ORDER WITH RESTRICTION

Summary A Crown Court orders (sentences) a person to hospital for treatment and in order to protect the public from serious harm a restriction is applied.

Legal criteria

Crown Court: a person is convicted of an offence punishable with imprisonment

and the person is suffering from mental illness, severe mental impairment psychopathic disorder or mental impairment

and the mental disorder is of a *nature or degree* which makes it appropriate for them to be detained in hospital for treatment
(for psychopathic disorder or mental impairment, such treatment is likely to alleviate or prevent a deterioration of their condition)

and the Court is of the opinion that the most suitable method of dealing with the person is by means of this order (Section 37)

and having regard to the nature of the offence, the offender's previous criminal record and the risk of them committing further offences if released, that it is necessary for the protection of the public from serious harm for special restrictions to apply (Section 41 restriction).

Powers
- *Detention* – the power to detain the person either for a set period of time or indefinitely.

- *Treatment* – the person can be given treatment for mental disorder with or without their consent (see page 64).

- *Absconding* – if the person absconds they can be forcibly returned to hospital by any authorised member of hospital staff or by the police. The Home Office should be informed immediately.

Who is involved? Two doctors - one of whom must be Section 12 approved (have experience of psychiatry) and one must give oral evidence before the Court. The doctors may work for the same NHS Trust.
and
the Crown Court – which makes the order.

Time limits The person must be admitted to hospital within 28 days of the order being made. If they are not admitted immediately, they can be detained for up to 28 days in a place of safety (for example prison) whilst a hospital bed is arranged.

Working With The Mental Health Act 1983

Leave of absence	The authority to grant leave rests with the Home Office, who produce an application form for consultants (RMOs) to request leave. The Home Office normally requires three weeks to consider a request for leave.
	Escorted leave for a person to attend Court for an alleged or proven offence or to attend another hospital for urgent medical treatment does not require prior Home Office approval, however they should be informed as soon as possible.
Patient rights	The right of appeal to the Mental Health Review Tribunal but only in the second six months of detention and then once a year.
	The right of appeal to the Hospital Managers, however they cannot discharge the person but only recommend discharge to the Home Office.
	The right of appeal to the Crown Court or Court of Appeal to have the conviction quashed or another sentence imposed.
	To right to be visited by and complain to the Mental Health Act Commission.
Duties on staff	Staff should take all practicable steps to ensure the patient understands their legal rights and provide this information both orally and in writing (*Patient Rights Leaflet 12*).
	The consultant (RMO) must provide yearly reports to the Home Office.
	The provision of after-care services under Section 117 upon discharge.
	The Home Office must refer the patient to a Mental Health Review Tribunal if their case has not been considered by the Tribunal in the previous three years.
Discharge	There are a number of ways for the section to end:
	❖ Discharge by a Mental Health Review Tribunal
	❖ Discharge by the Home Office, usually at the request of the consultant
	❖ Discharge by the Crown Court or Court of Appeal (this may result in the person being sentenced again but under criminal law)
	❖ A restriction order with a fixed time period expires. The section then becomes a normal Section 37 and begins from the date that the restriction order ends.
	Section 37/41 is often 'conditionally' discharged. This means the Section 37 ends but the Section 41 remains in effect (see *Section 41* on page 57).
Extending the section	It is not possible to extend the section because it is set for a fixed period of time (like a prison sentence) or for an indefinite period of time.
Forms	The Crown Court issues a Section 37/41 order.
Practical advice	A Magistrates' Court cannot make a Section 41 order, however, if it is making a Section 37 order and feels that a Section 41 is also required, it can transfer the case to a Crown Court.
Amending the Act	Section 37/41 will be partially affected by the planned changes to the definition of mental disorder, the abolition of the treatability test and the additional professionals who can undertake the role of responsible medical officer.

Working With The Mental Health Act 1983

SECTION 41
THE CONDITIONALLY DISCHARGED PATIENT

Summary Section 41 operates like a community section for people who were originally on Section 37/41. When a Section 37/41 is conditionally discharged it leaves the power of Section 41 in place. This means that the person can leave hospital and live in the community but with a number of conditions placed upon them. The section lasts for as long as the period of the original restriction order.

Legal criteria

Section 37/41 criteria (see page 55)

and the section is conditionally discharged by a
Mental Health Review Tribunal or the Home Office.

Powers The powers are flexible but generally include:

- *Residence* – the person is required to live at a specified place. However, they are not detained there.

- *Treatment* – the person is required to accept treatment. However, they can only be given treatment with their consent.

- *Supervision* – to keep appointments and agree access to a supervisor (normally an approved social worker or probation officer) and a consultant (RMO).

Failure to comply with the requirements of the order would lead to the Home Office being informed and the person could then be recalled to hospital. This would re-instate the powers of the original Section 37/41.

Who is involved? The Home Office or Mental Health Review Tribunal instigate the order by discharging Section 37 from a Section 37/41. They then impose a number of conditions on the person under the power of the remaining Section 41.
and
a community supervisor will be appointed for the person (often an approved social worker or probation officer). A consultant (RMO) will also be involved monitoring the person in the community.

Time limits The section lasts for as long as the original Section 41 order. This could be for an indefinite period of time.

Leave of absence If the person is required to live at specified premises they need permission from the Home Office to move or to take leave from this place.

Patient rights The right of appeal to the Mental Health Review Tribunal once during the 12 to 24 months after the conditional discharge and then once in every subsequent two year period.

To right to be visited by and complain to the Mental Health Act Commission.

Duties on staff	Although there is no specific rights leaflet for people who are conditionally discharged, staff should inform people of their rights under this section.

The community supervisor and consultant must provide reports to the Home Office on a regular basis. |
| **Discharge** | There are two ways for the section to end:

❖ Absolute discharge by the Mental Health Review Tribunal

❖ Absolute discharge by the Home Office |
| **Extending the section** | It is not possible to extend the section because it lasts for a fixed or indefinite period of time dictated by the Section 41 restriction. |
| **Forms** | A conditional discharge order from either the Home Office or Mental Health Review Tribunal. |
| **Practical advice** | The Home Office, under guidance from the community supervisor and the consultant, can recall the conditional discharge and the person would be re-admitted to hospital under the original powers of the Section 37/41. Once re-called the Home Office must refer the person's case for a Mental Health Review Tribunal hearing within a month of their admission to hospital.

The person can also be admitted to hospital as a voluntary patient or placed under a Section 2 or 3. In the event of such an admission to hospital the consultant must notify the Home Office promptly. |
| **Facts** | In 2004 the Home Office agreed to the conditional discharge of 43 people, whereas Mental Health Review Tribunals conditionally discharged 259 people[6].

Overall, the total number of conditionally discharged people in the community at any one time is approximately 1,200[7]. |
| **Amending the Act** | Section 41 will be partially affected by the additional professionals who can undertake the role of responsible medical officer. |

SECTION 47/49
TRANSFER FROM PRISON TO HOSPITAL WITH RESTRICTIONS

Summary   The transfer of a sentenced prisoner to hospital and their detention there (Section 47) with restrictions applied (Section 49) by the Home Office.

Legal criteria

The person is serving a sentence of imprisonment
and the Secretary of State is satisfied they are suffering from mental illness, severe mental impairment, psychopathic disorder or mental impairment

and the mental disorder is of a *nature or degree* which makes it appropriate for them to be detained in hospital for medical treatment (for psychopathic disorder or mental impairment, the treatment is likely to alleviate or prevent a deterioration of their condition)

and the Secretary of State, having regard to the public interest and all the circumstances, may direct that the person is removed to and detained in hospital (Section 47)

and having regard to the nature of the offence, the previous criminal record of the offender and the risk of them committing further offences if released, that it is necessary for the protection of the public from serious harm for special restrictions to apply (Section 49).

Powers
- *Detention* – the power to detain the person for as long as the restriction order is in place (that is the earliest date on which the prisoner may be discharged from prison) and thereafter as long as the Section 47 is in place.

- *Treatment* – the person can be given treatment for mental disorder with or without their consent (see page 64).

- *Absconding* – if the person absconds they can be forcibly returned to hospital by any authorised member of hospital staff or by the police. The Home Office must be informed immediately.

Who is involved?   Two doctors – one of whom must be Section 12 approved (have experience of psychiatry). Both doctors may work for the same NHS Trust.
and
the Home Office – which agrees and issues the transfer direction.

The Home Office is not obliged to agree to a Section 47/49 despite two medical recommendations being made. It will consider whether the prisoner can be safely contained by the hospital taking into account a number of risk factors including the nature of the offence, the length of the sentence and the risk of absconding.

Time limits   The person must be admitted to hospital within 14 days of the Section 47/49 being made.

Working With The Mental Health Act 1983

Leave of absence	The authority to grant leave rests with the Home Office and it will not normally be granted until the person is approaching their conditional, or non-parole, release date. Escorted leave for the person to attend Court for an alleged or proven offence or to attend another hospital for urgent medical treatment does not require prior Home Office approval, however they should be informed.
Patient rights	The right of appeal to the Mental Health Review Tribunal once in the first six months, once during the second six months and thereafter yearly.
	The right of appeal to the Hospital Managers, however they cannot discharge the person but only recommend discharge to the Home Office.
	The right to be visited by and complain to the Mental Health Act Commission.
Duties on staff	Staff should take all practicable steps to ensure the patient understands their legal rights and provide this information both orally and in writing (*Patient Rights Leaflet 18 + Home Office letter addressed to the person*).
	The provision of after-care services under Section 117 upon discharge.
	The consultant (RMO) must provide annual reports to the Home Office.
	The Home Office must refer the patient to the Mental Health Review Tribunal if their case has not been considered in the previous three years.
Discharge	There are a number of ways for the section to end:
	❖ Discharge by a Mental Health Review Tribunal (the person no longer requires treatment in hospital). The person would then return to prison unless the Home Office agreed to their discharge or the Tribunal ordered that they nonetheless remain in hospital.
	❖ The consultant (RMO) notifies the Home Office that the person no longer requires treatment in hospital or that no effective treatment can be given. The Home Office may then return the person to prison, release them on parole or allow the discharge.
	❖ If the person was subject to a fixed term sentence of imprisonment the restriction (Section 49) will terminate on the person's release date. The person is then only subject to Section 47 which operates like a Section 37.
Extending the section	It is not possible to extend the section because it runs for a fixed or indefinite period, set by the Section 49 restriction.
Forms	The Home Office issues a Section 47/49 transfer direction with restrictions. The two doctors making recommendations must agree on at least one form of mental disorder.
Code of Practice	The prison or remand centre should send the hospital a current medical report together with a report from the prison healthcare staff on the person's general care and also any relevant pre-sentence reports from the probation service.
Facts	Section 47/49 was used to transfer 299 people to hospital for the year ending March 2005[1].
Amending the Act	Section 47/49 will be partially affected by the planned changes to the definition of mental disorder, the abolition of the treatability test and the additional professionals who can undertake the role of responsible medical officer.

Working With The Mental Health Act 1983

SECTION 48/49
REMOVAL TO HOSPITAL OF OTHER PRISONERS WITH RESTRICTIONS

Summary
The transfer of an unsentenced prisoner to hospital and their detention there (Section 48) with restrictions applied by the Home Office (Section 49). If the person is involved in criminal proceedings, a restriction order is mandatory but for other cases, the Home Office will make an individual assessment of risk.

Legal criteria

An unsentenced prisoner who is either detained in prison or a remand centre, or remanded in custody by a Magistrates' Court, or committed to prison by a Court for a limited term, or detained under the Immigration Act 1971 (or Section 62 of the Nationality, Immigration and Asylum Act 2002)

and the Secretary of State is satisfied that the person is suffering from mental illness or severe mental impairment of a *nature or degree* which makes it appropriate for them to be detained and treated in hospital

and the person is in urgent need of such treatment (Section 48)

and having regard to the nature of the offence, the previous criminal record of the offender and the risk of them committing further offences if released, that it is necessary for the protection of the public from serious harm for special restrictions to apply (Section 49).

Powers
- *Detention* – the power to detain the person for a period of time as given by the restriction order.

- *Treatment* – the person can be given treatment for mental disorder with or without their consent (see page 64).

- *Absconding* – if the person absconds they can be forcibly returned to hospital by any authorised member of hospital staff or by the police. The Home Office must be informed immediately.

Who is involved?
Two doctors – one of whom must be Section 12 approved (have experience of psychiatry). Both doctors may work for the same NHS Trust.
and
the Home Office – which agrees and issues the transfer direction.

It is important to note that the Home Office is not obliged to agree to a Section 48/49 despite two medical recommendations being made. It will consider whether the prisoner can be safely contained by the hospital, taking into account a number of risk factors including the nature of the offence, their behaviour in prison and the risk of absconding.

Time limits
The person must be admitted to hospital within 14 days of the Section 48/49 being issued.

Leave of absence	The authority to grant leave rests with the Home Office. Leave is not normally granted unless there are exceptional grounds for doing so. Escorted leave for a person to attend Court for an alleged or proven offence or to attend another hospital for urgent medical treatment does not require prior Home Office approval, however they should be informed as soon as possible.
Patient rights	The right of appeal to the Mental Health Review Tribunal, once in the first six months, once in the second six months and thereafter yearly. The right of appeal to the Hospital Managers, however they cannot discharge the person but only recommend discharge to the Home Office. The right to be visited by and complain to the Mental Health Act Commission.
Duties on staff	Staff should take all practicable steps to ensure the patient understands their legal rights and provide this information both orally and in writing (*Patient Rights Leaflet 20 and a Home Office letter addressed to the person*). The provision of after-care services under Section 117 upon discharge.
Discharge	There are a number of ways for the section to end: ❖ When the Court proceedings in connection with the section are complete. ❖ For patients under Section 48/49 remanded in custody by a Magistrates' Court, the restriction order ends at the expiration of the period of remand unless the person is then committed in custody to the Crown Court. ❖ For patients under Section 48/49 who are civil prisoners or immigration detainees the section ends on the expiration of the original detention period. ❖ Discharge by a Mental Health Review Tribunal. The person will then be detained under the criminal justice system as before, while the Court considers the next course of action. ❖ If the consultant (RMO) reports to the Home Office that the person no longer requires treatment in hospital or that no effective treatment can be given, the person will be detained under the criminal justice system as before.
Extending the section	The section can only be extended by the Court imposing another section (Section 37 or 37/41) at the end of the trial.
Forms	The Home Office issues a Section 48/49 transfer direction order with restriction.
Code of Practice	Upon transfer, the prison or remand centre should send the hospital a current medical report together with a report from the prison healthcare staff on the person's general care and also any relevant pre-sentence reports from the probation service.
Facts	Section 48/49 is the second most used forensic section and the most used restricted section. For the year ending March 2005 it was applied 346 times[6].
Amending the Act	Section 48/49 will be partially affected by the planned changes to the definition of mental disorder and the additional professionals who can undertake the role of responsible medical officer.

SUMMARY OF TREATMENT UNDER THE MENTAL HEALTH ACT

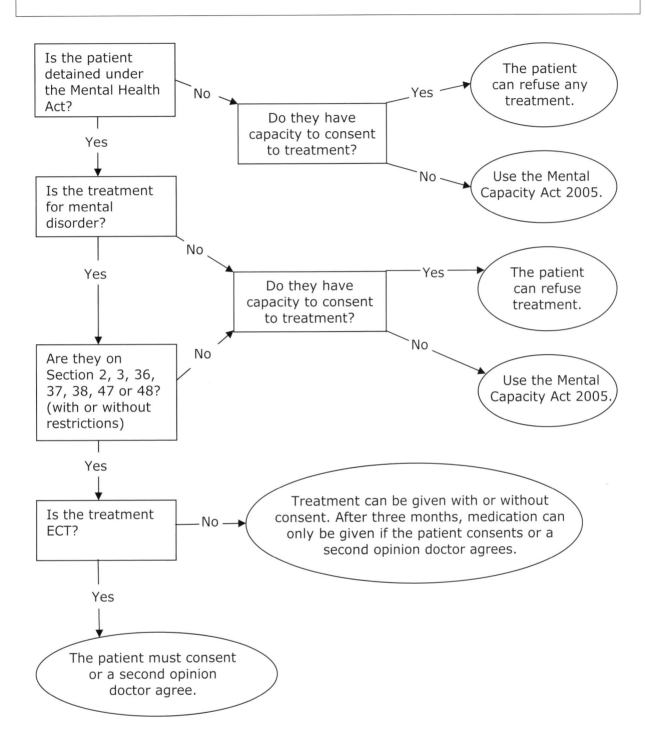

Note: If psychosurgery or the implantation of hormones is proposed as treatment then the patient must consent and a second opinion doctor plus two other independent people must also agree. This applies to both detained and informal (voluntary) patients.

Working With The Mental Health Act 1983

TREATMENT POWERS

The power to give treatment with or without consent is contained in Part IV of the Act (Consent to Treatment). Sections 56 to 64, within Part IV, detail the powers to treat people under the Act and the rules and limitations that apply to these powers.

Limitations

The treatment powers listed below are limited in a number of ways:

- *Detained patients on short-term or community sections are excluded:*

Therefore patients under Sections 4, 5(2), 5(4), 7 (guardianship), 25 (supervised discharge), 35, 37 (guardianship), 41 only (conditionally discharged), 135(1) and 136, are not subject to these powers of the Act and can only be given treatment with their consent.

- *Only treatment for mental disorder is allowed:*

Treatment for mental disorder allows a broad range of treatments including medication for mental disorder or care under medical supervision to alleviate the symptoms of the disorder. It also includes nursing care or monitoring blood where this is part of taking certain medication. In addition diagnostic tests for mental disorder and the care provided whilst a patient is in seclusion are covered. General medical treatment may also be given if it can be shown to be treating a symptom directly resulting from the person's mental disorder or integral to it. For example, the use of nasal-gastric tube feeding in the case of someone with anorexia nervosa.

- *Some treatments require special procedures to be followed.*

Treatment without consent (Section 63)

Section 63 of the Act provides the power to give treatment to detained patients with or without their consent.

The key limitations on this power are:

✓ Only patients on long-term sections can be given such treatment (Sections 2, 3, 36, 37 (hospital order), 38, 47 and 48 (with or without restrictions)

✓ Treatment is only for mental disorder.

✓ Some treatments are excluded – electro convulsive therapy (ECT), psychosurgery and the surgical implantation of hormones.

✓ For medication, the power lasts for three months. After this, the person must either consent or a second opinion approved doctor (SOAD) appointed by the Mental Health Act Commission must agree to the treatment.

Although the three month period should begin when medication is first given, it is common practice to start it from the time a person is detained (not including the short-term sections listed earlier which are excluded from this part of the Act), which may be an earlier date than when the medication began.

Treatment requiring consent or a second opinion (Section 58)

Treatment covered by Section 58 of the Act can only be given if a detained patient consents or if they do not consent then a second opinion approved doctor must agree to the treatment instead. This section covers the following treatments:

• *the use of electro convulsive therapy (ECT) at any time*

For ECT to be given at *any time* during detention the patient must either consent and their consultant (RMO) complete a Form 38 or a second opinion approved doctor (SOAD) must be called to complete a Form 39 authorising treatment for patients who do not or cannot consent.

• *medication for mental disorder after three months*

After medication has been given for three months (under the powers of Section 63) Section 58 comes into force. It provides a means of protection for patients being treated. After three months, a detained patient must either consent to treatment or a second opinion approved doctor (SOAD) be called. If the patient consents to treatment the consultant (RMO) must complete Form 38 stating the patient has understood the nature, purpose and likely effects of the treatment and consented to it.

If the patient refuses treatment or does not have capacity to consent then a second opinion approved doctor must be called. They will consult a nurse who has been involved with the patient, another professional who is not a nurse or doctor, the consultant and the patient. Following these consultations the second opinion doctor, having regard to the likelihood of treatment alleviating or preventing deterioration in the condition of the patient, can authorise the treatment using Form 39.

Note: a patient may initially consent to treatment and a Form 38 is signed. However, they can later refuse treatment at any time which would invalidate the Form 38 and treatment must stop. A second opinion approved doctor should then be called. If needed, during the interim period, emergency treatment may be considered under Section 62. Form 38 would also become invalid if the person lost their capacity to consent to treatment or if the treatment prescribed was different to that originally written on the Form 38.

Special treatment requiring consent and a second opinion (Section 57)

Section 57 of the Act concerns special treatment that requires additional procedures to be followed before it can be given. Note: in contrast to all the other treatment rules, this section applies to both detained and informal (voluntary) patients. The special treatments are:

- *surgery to destroy brain tissue or the functioning of brain tissue (psychosurgery)*

- *other treatment as specified by regulations made by the Secretary of State for Health. To date this has been the surgical implantation of hormones to reduce male sex drive.*

To carry out either of the above treatments the patient MUST consent and a second opinion approved doctor and two other independent people (appointed by the Mental Health Act Commission) must agree that the patient has capacity to consent to the treatment. In addition, the second opinion approved doctor must consult with two staff who are involved with the patient's treatment (at least one nurse and one other professional who is not a nurse or doctor) before agreeing that the treatment should be given.

Urgent treatment (Section 62)

Section 62 of the Act authorises the administration of treatment in circumstances where the procedures for Section 57 or 58 (special treatment and consent or a second opinion) cannot be followed because there is an urgent need to give the treatment.

Urgent treatment is defined as:

- treatment which is immediately necessary to save the patient's life.

- treatment which (not being irreversible) is immediately necessary to prevent a serious deterioration of the patient's condition.

- treatment which (not being irreversible or hazardous) is immediately necessary to alleviate serious suffering to the patient.

- treatment which (not being irreversible or hazardous) is immediately necessary and represents the minimum interference necessary to prevent the patient from behaving violently or being a danger to themselves or to others.

- treatment where a patient that has previously consented withdraws their consent and the consultant (RMO) considers that stopping treatment would cause serious suffering to the patient.

The Act defines "irreversible" as treatment that has unfavourable irreversible physical or psychological consequences. "Hazardous" is defined as treatment that entails significant physical hazard.

Section 62 is designed to allow emergency treatment in circumstances where the other treatment powers cannot be used. However, other treatment powers of the Act should be brought into place swiftly to end the need for Section 62. An example of its use is when ECT is needed as a matter of urgency and the patient does not consent. Section 62 could be applied to give ECT immediately whilst arrangements are made for a second opinion doctor to see the patient as required under Section 58 to authorise the treatment.

As with other treatment powers, Section 62 only relates to detained patients on long-term sections. There is no statutory form for using Section 62 so each NHS Trust should produce its own.

Patients on leave

Patients detained under a section but granted leave of absence are still covered by the treatment powers of the Act so the rules and procedures as given above apply to them.

Review of treatment (Section 61)

Section 61 places a duty on the consultant (RMO) to regularly review the treatment of patients for whom a second opinion approved doctor has authorised treatment. The review requires the consultant to complete Form MHAC1 whenever the patient's section is extended (renewed), when requested by the Mental Health Act Commission or for restricted patients six months after the section began and then yearly. The MHAC1 should be sent to the Mental Health Act Commission and the patient should also be given a copy.

Case Law

The Courts have ruled that where a person has capacity to refuse treatment but is detained under the Mental Health Act, treatment for mental disorder can be given without consent and this does not conflict with the Human Rights Act.

In the case concerned, PS was detained in hospital under the Act. It was accepted that he had capacity to give or withhold consent to treatment. PS argued that compulsory treatment would breach the prohibition on torture and inhuman and degrading treatment under Article 3 of the European Convention on Human Rights and his right to respect for his private life under Article 8.

However, the Court did not agree and stated that capacity is only one of the factors to be taken into account when deciding what is medically necessary and in the best interests of the patient. Therefore, a competent *detained* patient can be forced to accept medical treatment for mental disorder even if they oppose the treatment.

(From the case of: R (on the application of PS) v (1) Dr G and (2) Dr W [2003] EWHC 2335 (Admin), September 2003)

Further information

The Mental Health Act Commission has produced a number of guidance notes concerning treatment (see page 123).

LEAVE OF ABSENCE

A detained patient may not leave hospital unless granted leave under Section 17 of the Act (or Section 19 if being transferred to another hospital).

Rules

- ✓ A consultant (RMO) may grant leave to most patients detained under the Act.

- ✓ A consultant may NOT grant leave to restricted patients without the prior approval of the Home Office.

- ✓ A consultant may NOT grant leave to patients under Section 35, 36 or 38.

- ✓ The leave may be granted with or without conditions, as considered appropriate by the consultant, in the interests of the patient or for the protection of others.

- ✓ The consultant may direct that the patient be escorted by another person during their leave for the protection of the patient or others. In this case, the patient can be escorted by a member of hospital staff or another person as authorised in writing by the consultant.

Generally, no formalities are required should a detained patient need to go to different parts of the hospital or hospital grounds. Leave may be extended in the absence of the patient if it is for a specified period.

Purpose

Leave can be granted for a specific period of time, such as a weekend, or for a specific occasion, such as a family celebration.

Code of Practice

The Code gives the following guidance:

- ➢ The consultant cannot delegate the decision to grant leave. However, if the consultant is absent, for example due to leave or illness, the doctor in charge of the patient's treatment during that time can grant leave. Where possible this should be another consultant, locum consultant or specialist registrar approved under Section 12 of the Act.

- ➢ The Hospital Managers cannot overrule a decision to grant leave.

Planning and consultation

The Code of Practice emphasises that leave should be well planned and provide an opportunity to assess how the patient would manage if discharged. The patient should be involved in the decision to grant leave and, with the patient's consent, relatives, carers and friends should be consulted, especially if the patient is to reside with them during their leave. A patient should not be granted leave if they do not consent to such consultation where the consultation is with relatives, carers or friends who are to be involved in their care.

Working With The Mental Health Act 1983

Short-term leave

The consultant can grant short-term periods of leave which can be given at the discretion of nursing staff. However, the leave must be taken within the period originally granted by the consultant. The consultant should continue to review the leave regularly and this should be recorded in the patient's notes.

Records

There is no statutory leave of absence form so each NHS Trust should produce one. A copy should be given to the patient and all those involved in their care.

Duty of care

The consultant remains responsible for the patient's care and treatment while they are on leave. The duty to provide after-care services under Section 117 includes detained patients on leave.

Where a patient does not consent to medication, while on leave, they can be recalled to hospital in order to administer medication under Part IV of the Act (Consent to Treatment).

Another hospital

Leave can also be used to allow a patient to stay in another hospital if required, for example for medical treatment. However, if such leave continues for an extended period of time, a transfer of the section to the other hospital should be considered (see page 84).

Case Law

Case 1 – CS had been on continuous leave for three months during which time her Section 3 was extended (renewed) by her consultant (RMO). During her leave she only came to hospital for a ward round once a month. She appealed to the Mental Health Review Tribunal for discharge and was unsuccessful. She then appealed against the Tribunal's decision but this was dismissed by the Court. The consultant (RMO) argued that long-term leave was a way of facilitating early discharge from detention. The consultant could only 'risk' the discharge of the patient in accordance with her own judgment. The Court also noted the importance of the section in allowing the clinical team to bring the patient back as soon as there were signs of deterioration. It was reasoned that this resulted in minimal periods of detention, reducing distress to CS and the damage to the relationship between her and the clinical team.

(From the case of: R (on the application of CS) v Mental Health Review Tribunal and Managers of Homerton Hospital (East London & City Mental Health NHS Trust) [2004] EWHC 2958 (admin))

Case 2 – A consultant's (RMO) authority to grant leave does not extend to a duty upon the NHS to provide funding to facilitate the patient's use of their leave. A consultant will decide to grant leave of absence on the basis of the risk to the patient or others, they should not also have to consider financial constraints.

(From the case of: R v West London Mental Health NHS Trust 2006 (CA))

Further information

The Mental Health Act Commission has produced a guidance note on leave (see page 123). The Home Office has also produced a guide to leave for people on forensic restricted sections (see page 53).

REVOKING (RECALLING) LEAVE OF ABSENCE

A consultant (RMO) can revoke (recall) a patient's leave of absence under Section 17(4) if it is considered necessary in the interests of the patient's health or safety or for the protection of others.

Procedure

- In order to recall a patient, notice in writing must be served on them or on the person in charge of the patient while they are on leave.

- The reasons for the recall should be explained to the patient and the explanation should be recorded in their notes.

Time limits

Leave of absence cannot be revoked if a person is no longer liable to be detained under the Act or has been on leave continuously for more than 12 months, whichever is earlier.

Recall of restricted patients

For patients on restricted Sections 37/41, 47/49 and 48/49 either a consultant (RMO) or the Home Office can revoke leave. However, the patient cannot be recalled if the period of detention has expired.

Relatives, carers, friends and professionals involved with the patient should contact the patient's consultant if they believe the patient should return to hospital before their leave is due to end.

ABSENCE WITHOUT LEAVE

Section 18 of the Act provides the power to retake a patient detained under the legislation who has gone absent without leave (AWOL).

Criteria

The Act states that for patients who are detained, the following actions make a person absent without leave:

> Leaving hospital without being granted leave
> Failing to return to hospital after a period of authorised leave has expired
> Failing to return to hospital after being recalled from a period of authorised leave
> Being absent without authority from the address they are required to reside at, for example as a condition of their leave or under terms imposed by their guardian

Taking into custody

The following people can take a patient who is absent without leave into custody and return them to a specified address or hospital:

> An approved social worker
> A member of hospital staff (including staff of a hospital the patient is required to reside at as a condition of their leave)
> A police officer
> A person authorised in writing by the Hospital Managers
> A member of staff from another hospital if authorised by the Hospital Managers of the detaining hospital

> For guardianship the following people are authorised: local authority (social services) staff, a police officer or any person authorised by the guardian or local authority

Entering locked premises

Although the Act provides the legal authority to retake a detained patient who is absent without leave, the patient may be in private premises and prevent access. In these circumstances staff would need to apply to a magistrate for a Section 135(2) warrant (see page 17). This provides the additional authority to forcibly enter private locked premises and retake a detained patient who is absent without leave.

Patients taken to another hospital

If a patient who is absent without leave is taken to another hospital, the hospital may be given the authority in writing by the original detaining hospital to detain the patient in the short-term until arrangements are made for their return.

Patients subject to short-term powers

Patients who are absent without leave under one of the following short-term sections cannot be taken into custody if that section has expired - Sections 2, 4, 5(2), 5(4), 135(1) and 136.

Patients subject to long-term powers

The Mental Health (Patients in the Community) Act 1995 amended the original powers of the Mental Health Act concerning patients who are absent without leave and changed the time limits previously set to return such patients.

Patients who are absent without leave and on Sections 3, 7, 37 (both hospital order and guardianship order) and 47 can be returned:

> ➢ up to six months after going absent without leave
> **or**
> ➢ until the expiry date of the section they are under

The later date of the above two will be the relevant date. If a person returns after being absent without leave for more than 28 days, a number of procedural steps have to be taken. For full details see the *Memorandum* to the Act available at *www.markwalton.net.*

Patients subject to restriction orders

Patients on restricted Sections 37/41, 47/49 and 48/49 are not subject to time limits and can be retaken for as long as their section is in force. The Home Office must be informed immediately when any restricted patient goes absent without leave.

Retaking patients outside England and Wales

Section 88 allows the retaking of patients while they are in any part of the United Kingdom, Isle of Man or Channel Islands. It applies only to patients who are absent without leave from a hospital in England and Wales.

Patients absent without leave may be retaken by:

> ➢ any person who has authority to retake them in England and Wales
> ➢ those equivalent to approved social workers in Scotland or Northern Ireland
> ➢ a police officer in the country in which they are found

However, this does not apply to those subject to guardianship.

Criminal offence

It is a criminal offence under Section 128 of the Act to induce or assist a person who is detained to go absent without leave from hospital. In addition, it is also an offence to knowingly harbour a person who is absent without leave from hospital.

A patient wishing to appeal against their detention may do so in one of two ways:

> ➢ appeal to a Mental Health Review Tribunal (see page 76).
>   **or**
> ➢ appeal to the Hospital Managers (see page 80).

Not all sections may be appealed against. To see which can, look under *Patient rights* in each section as given earlier.

Some hearings take place not because a patient has appealed but due to automatic appeal processes which take place on their behalf when they have not appealed for certain periods of time or when their section is extended (renewed).

Limits

A patient may appeal to a Tribunal once in every period of detention. However, there is no limit to the number of times someone may appeal to the Hospital Managers.

Withdrawing an appeal

If a patient wishes to withdraw their appeal after it has been made, they may do so by putting the request in writing. It is at the discretion of the Tribunal or the Hospital Managers whether they accept the withdrawal request. They may ask the patient's solicitor to confirm the details or may decide to proceed with the hearing regardless.

Location

Tribunal and Hospital Managers' hearings will normally be conducted in a room within the hospital grounds. The patient and ward will be notified of the time and location.

Constitution

A Tribunal panel consists of three people:

- *President*. The person seated in the centre is the legal member and is called the president, they will act much like a chairperson during the hearing.

- *Medical member*. The medical member will be a consultant psychiatrist and will have already met with the patient prior to the hearing.

- *Lay member*. This person does not necessarily hold any legal or medical qualifications however, they should have general experience in mental health.

In Hospital Managers' hearings, the three members will generally not be medically or legally trained.

Nearest relative and carers

With the patient's consent, their nearest relative or most concerned relatives should be informed of the hearing. Relatives and carers may be invited to express their views to the panel. However, if the patient objects to this, an appropriate member of the professional team should be asked to incorporate these views into their report.

The patient may invite anyone they would like to attend the hearing with them.

Reports

Before the hearing takes place, written reports should be produced (see page 81).

Procedure

Although the format of a hearing may vary, the following procedure is the general way in which hearings are conducted.

> ➤ Each person at the hearing including the panel, will introduce themselves.
> ➤ The patient should be given the opportunity to explain their reasons for requesting discharge (if they have).
> ➤ The patient should be allowed a friend or representative they have chosen to help and support them when they put their views to the panel.
> ➤ The consultant (RMO) and other professionals should explain why they believe the patient's continued detention is justified.
> ➤ All parties at the hearing (including the patient if they want this to be the case) should be able to hear each other's statements and to put questions to each other.
> ➤ The patient should be offered the opportunity of speaking to the panel in private.

The order of witnesses will usually be as follows:

- consultant (RMO)
- approved social worker or care co-ordinator
- nurse
- patient

Each witness will usually be asked to summarise their report and then answer any questions the panel may have for them. They will then be questioned by the patient's legal representative or the patient if they have decided to represent themselves. Finally, a closing argument is given by the patient or their legal representative before the panel retire to consider their verdict.

Etiquette

The appropriate form of address for the chairperson or president of a hearing is 'Sir' or 'Madam'. When a witness is giving evidence, the other witnesses should remain silent. The hearing itself is relatively informal and witnesses give evidence while seated.

Legal representation

It should be noted that the style of advocacy used by legal representatives should not be adversarial as with most other legal hearings in this country. Instead, the purpose of the hearing is to get a balanced and accurate picture of the patient and therefore the advocacy should be conducted in an inquisitorial style. That is, the focus of all parties should be to establish the actual facts of the situation as objectively as possible, as opposed to trying to place blame on either party.

Patients are entitled to free legal representation at Tribunals regardless of their financial circumstances. Hospitals should ensure they have an up-to-date list of solicitors approved by the Law Society to represent patients at Tribunals. The Tribunal may adjourn a hearing where a patient is not legally represented and ask that such representation is organised to ensure the patient has the best opportunity to present their case. Automatic free legal representation at Hospital Managers' hearings is not available, however many solicitors offer such support and a patient should discuss this with their solicitor.

After-care arrangements

In the event of a Hospital Managers' or Tribunal hearing being minded to discharge a patient, they need to consider arrangements for their after-care following discharge. If these have yet to be made, it may be appropriate to adjourn for a brief period to allow for a Care Programme Approach (CPA) meeting to take place.

Delayed (deferred) discharge

A hearing may decide to order the delayed discharge of a patient. This can be used to allow arrangements to be made prior the patient being discharged, for example ensuring that appropriate housing will be available. A delayed discharge can state a specific date in the future when the patient will be discharged from section. The Tribunal, for forensic restricted patients, can make a general requirement of conditions that must be met without a specific time limit attached, such as the provision of housing, before the discharge will take place.

The decision

In practice, in addition to the statutory criteria, the panel's main concerns will be:

> ➤ Does the applicant accept their condition and generally show insight into the mental disorder?
> ➤ Is the detained person co-operative with mental health services and is their compliance likely to continue after discharge?
> ➤ Is the detained person compliant with taking medication and is this likely to continue after discharge?
> ➤ Is there any distinction between what can be done for the person in hospital or can they be as effectively treated at home? (For example, with support from carers).

The decision of the panel and their reasons for it must be recorded and placed in the patient's records. The patient and all those attending the hearing should be informed of the decision in writing. The nearest relative should also be informed with the patient's consent. At least one member of the panel should meet with the patient to give them the decision in person and explain the reasoning behind it.

Case Law

The Courts have ruled that in a decision to discharge a person from section, the three members of a Tribunal or Hospital Managers' hearing must all agree.

(From the case of: R (On the application of Fredrick Tagoe-Thompson) v Hospital Managers of Park Royal centre sub nov Central and North West London Mental Heath NHS Trust (2003) EWCA Civ 330)

Appealing against the decision of a hearing

In order to appeal against a decision of the Tribunal or Hospital Mangers, an application for judicial review must be made.

There is a right of appeal to the Mental Health Review Tribunal for many detained patients and their nearest relatives. In addition, hospitals and care homes that detain patients have a duty to refer cases to the Tribunal when a patient has not had a Tribunal hearing for a certain period of time (see the individual sections for further information).

Contact

Mental Health Review Tribunal
5th Floor, 11 Belgrave Road, Victoria, London SW1V 1RS.

Tel: 020 7592 1044 & 1017 Fax: 020 7592 1084 Website: www.mhrt.org.uk

Facts

The Tribunal has a considerable workload and for the year ending March 2005 it received 22,000 individual appeals. This resulted in almost 12,000 actual Tribunal hearings with a discharge rate of 15% [9].

Powers of Tribunals

Sections 72 to 74 of the Act give the criteria which must be met before a Tribunal may discharge a patient. The discharge criteria vary in accordance with the section under which a patient is detained. The Tribunal makes its decisions based on the civil standard of proof, this is on the balance of probabilities, what is more likely than not.

Procedure

At the start of the Tribunal, the president will ask the consultant (RMO) the statutory questions which must be satisfied. These questions are to establish whether the section criteria under which the person is detained are still satisfied. If they are not, the Tribunal may discharge immediately.

Discharge criteria – Section 2

In relation to people detained under Section 2, the Tribunal should discharge them if they are satisfied that:

> the person is not suffering from a mental disorder
> **or**
> the mental disorder is not of a nature or degree which warrants detention in hospital for assessment or assessment followed by treatment
> **or**
> detention is not justified in the interests of the person's own health or safety or for the protection of others.

Discharge criteria – Sections 3, 37, 47 and 48

If a person is detained under Section 3, 37, 47 or 48, the Tribunal should discharge them if they are satisfied that:

> the person is not suffering from mental illness, psychopathic disorder, severe mental impairment or mental impairment
> **or**

any of those forms of disorder are not of a nature or degree which makes it appropriate for them to be detained in hospital for medical treatment

or

it is not necessary for the health or safety of the patient or for the protection of others that they should receive such treatment

or

for Section 3, if the nearest relative has applied to discharge the patient and this has been barred by the consultant (RMO), that the patient, if released, would not be likely to act in a manner dangerous to themselves or others.

Other discharge criteria

The Tribunal must consider the additional statutory criteria that relate to some sections when making their decision.

Where a person has psychopathic disorder or mental impairment under the Act, treatment must be likely to alleviate or prevent a deterioration of the person's condition. This requirement also forms part of the criteria for the extension (renewal) of Section 3, 37 or 47 for all four mental disorders used by the Act. Alternatively the criteria for extension (renewal) of Section 3, 37 or 47 where the person suffers from mental illness or severe mental impairment, can also be the likelihood of the patient, if discharged, being unable to care for themselves, to obtain the care they need, or to guard themselves against serious exploitation.

Discharge criteria – guardianship

If a person is under guardianship, the Tribunal can order their discharge if they are satisfied that:

they are not suffering from mental illness, psychopathic disorder, severe mental impairment or mental impairment

or

it is not necessary in the interests of the welfare of the patient or for the protection of other persons that they should remain under such guardianship.

Discharge criteria – supervised discharge

If a person is under supervised discharge, the Tribunal can order their discharge if they are satisfied that:

they are not suffering from mental illness, mental impairment, severe mental impairment or psychopathic disorder

or

there is not a *substantial* risk of *serious* harm to the health or safety of the person or the safety of others or that the person will be seriously exploited if they do not receive the after-care services to be provided for them after they leave hospital under supervised discharge

and

being subject to supervised discharge will not be likely to help them receive aftercare services.

Discharge criteria – forensic restricted sections

Under Section 73, the Tribunal should order the absolute discharge of a restricted patient where they are satisfied that:

the patient is not suffering from mental illness, psychopathic disorder, severe mental impairment or mental impairment

or

any of the forms of disorder are not of a nature or degree which makes it appropriate for them to be detained in hospital for medical treatment
and
it is not appropriate for the patient to remain liable to be recalled to hospital for further treatment.

If a patient is *absolutely* discharged they are no longer liable to be detained under the hospital order which had applied to them and the restriction order they were subject to will also no longer apply.

The Tribunal should *conditionally* discharge restricted patients where the criteria are satisfied but they consider that the patient should still be liable to be recalled (Section 41 only, see page 57). The patient must comply with the conditions of the discharge set by the Tribunal or the Home Office while conditionally discharged. The Home Office has the power to vary the conditions imposed.

The Tribunal also has the power to defer a direction for conditional discharge until such arrangements, as appear necessary to them, for the discharge have been met. For example, appropriate housing in the community.

Unlike non-restricted patients, even if a restricted patient's condition is not being treated or alleviated, the Tribunal cannot automatically discharge the patient.

Additional factors – Sections 47/49 and 48/49

In the case of patients under Sections 47/49 and 48/49 the Tribunal, upon an appeal being made, should notify the Home Office whether the patient, if subject to a restriction order, is entitled to be absolutely or conditionally discharged. Further, they may propose that if the patient cannot be conditionally discharged contrary to the Tribunal's recommendation, then their detention continues in hospital.

Where the Tribunal recommends discharge, the Home Office has 90 days to notify the Tribunal whether the patient may be discharged in accordance with their recommendation. In the absence of such notice by the Home Office or an alternative direction by the Tribunal, the hospital should transfer the patient to a prison or other institution in which they might have been detained if they had not been removed to hospital under the Act. The patient will then be dealt with there as if they had not been removed.

Additional factors – Sections 47 and 48

In the case of patients detained under Section 48, where the Tribunal notifies the Home Office that the patient would be entitled to absolute or conditional discharge, in the absence of a recommendation by the Tribunal, the Home Office shall direct that the patient be sent to a prison or other institution in which they might have been detained (if they had not been removed to hospital), to be dealt with as if they had not been removed.

Where a Section 47 patient is still liable to serve their sentence following discharge by a Tribunal, the Tribunal must inform the Home Office of the discharge and may also recommend that the patient stay in hospital instead of returning to prison. Alternatively the Home Office may agree to a sentenced prisoner's discharge, in which case the patient will not have to be returned to prison.

Recommendations

Even if the Tribunal does not order discharge, they may make recommendations with a view to encouraging or facilitating a patient's future discharge:

> - recommending leave of absence
> - recommending transfer to another hospital
> - recommending transfer into guardianship
> - recommending that the patient's case be considered further in the event of any of their recommendations not being complied with

General powers

The Tribunal has the following general powers:

- ✓ the power to obtain any information they consider necessary
- ✓ the power to summon witnesses
- ✓ the medical member has the power (and is required) to examine the patient

Any other doctor authorised by the patient may also examine the patient in private and inspect records relating to the patient's detention or treatment in hospital.

Case Law

Re-detention of patients after discharge by the Tribunal

The case concerned a patient who had been granted deferred (delayed) discharge from Section 2 by a Tribunal but was then detained again under Section 3 the day before the discharge was due to take effect. At the House of Lords the judge, Lord Bingham, came to the following conclusions and declared that the detention under Section 3 was valid:

- ✓ A Tribunal can only decide upon the patient's condition at the time of the hearing and consider the foreseeable consequences of discharge.
- ✓ The Tribunal cannot make an assessment guaranteed to be accurate indefinitely or for any pre-determined period of time.
- ✓ A psychiatrist who has an opinion should not oppose or suppress that opinion because it does not comply with that of the Tribunal.
- ✓ An approved social worker should not apply for the detention of a patient who has been discharged by the Tribunal "....unless the approved social worker forms the reasonable and *bona fide* opinion that they have information not known to the Tribunal which puts a significantly different complexion on the case as compared with that which was before the Tribunal".

(From the case of: R V East London and the City Mental Health Trust and another, ex parte von Brandenburg [2-3] UKHL 58. November 2003)

Amending the Act

One of the government's proposed amendments to the Act is designed to increase the frequency and speed of Tribunals (see page 97).

The term 'Hospital Managers' as used in the Act, refers to the NHS Trust (or other body such as a private hospital or care home) which detains a person. The legislation gives the Hospital Managers a number of duties and powers, the most prominent of which is the discharge of detained patients. This power and others can be delegated to a committee which consists of people who are appointed to act as managers but are not employees of the NHS Trust. They are therefore able to make independent decisions.

A Hospital Managers' hearing is very similar in procedure to a Mental Health Review Tribunal (see page 73). However, in contrast to the Tribunal there is no requirement for the panel to contain legally or medically qualified members. The Hospital Managers' panel should contain at least three members who have appropriate experience and training.

Hospital Managers' hearings *may* take place:

✓ at any time at the Hospital Managers' discretion.

Hearings *must* take place:

✓ when a consultant (RMO) submits a report extending (renewing) a patient's section, even if the patient does not object to the renewal.

Hearings *must be considered:*

✓ at the patient's request
or
✓ if the consultant (RMO) under Section 25(1) submits a report stopping a nearest relative's application to discharge the patient.

The Hospital Managers may consider refusing a patient's request for a hearing when the following conditions are met:

✓ a hearing has already taken place in the last 28 days
and
✓ there is a lack of evidence to suggest that there has been a change in the patient's condition
or
✓ a Mental Health Review Tribunal is due to take place in the next 28 days

Limitation of Hospital Managers

The members of the panel are not in a position to make their own clinical judgments (as they do not have a medical member) and consequently, in the event of a difference of opinion, they should consider adjourning the matter in order to seek further medical or other professional advice.

Discharge criteria

The legal criteria applied by the Hospital Managers are not stated in the Act but essentially will mirror that of the Mental Health Review Tribunal.

Duties

The NHS Trust or hospital authority has the ultimate obligation to ensure the proper exercise of the Hospital Managers' powers of review. In the case of care homes the person or persons registered as owners hold that obligation.

Many professionals will be required to write a report at some point for use in Mental Health Act hearings. Most commonly, approved social workers and consultants (RMOs) write reports on patients in advance of hearings. Nurses may also write reports although these are generally less formal in nature.

The Mental Health Review Tribunal has produced guidance for professionals writing reports. An outline of that guidance is given below. However, for further information see *www.mhrt.org.uk.*

Social circumstances reports

Key Information

- date of birth
- date of current section
- section
- hospital
- ward
- their address at the time of admission

Content

The report should give full details of:

- ✓ the patient's home and family circumstances
- ✓ the views of the patient's nearest relative (or the person acting in that capacity)
- ✓ any employment opportunities
- ✓ what housing would be available upon discharge
- ✓ what community support will be available
- ✓ the financial circumstances of the patient
- ✓ the view of the social worker on whether the patient should be discharged

Medical reports

Key Information

- name
- section
- date section will expire
- name of the consultant and the doctor making the report (with their job title if they are not the consultant)
- the care co-ordinator

Content

The report should give full details of:

- ✓ the circumstances surrounding the patient's detention
- ✓ the nature and degree of the patient's mental disorder
- ✓ the reason for detention, based on the legal criteria of the section
- ✓ why detention is necessary, as opposed to treatment in the community or another alternative to hospital which may be less restrictive
- ✓ any other relevant and significant history
- ✓ any progress since admission including: leave, insight and compliance, both now and expected compliance in the future

Working With The Mental Health Act 1983

- ✓ the patient's current medication
- ✓ any medication which is being tried
- ✓ the patient's unmet needs
- ✓ the consequences of discharge, including risk and how it may be dealt with in the environment the patient may be discharged to
- ✓ details of any after-care being considered

In addition to the above list, there are further considerations in relation to restricted patients.

Information not to be disclosed to the patient

A consultant, social worker, nurse or other person producing a report for a hearing may request that certain information is not disclosed to the patient. This should be written as a separate report to the main one. However, it is for the Hospital Managers or the Tribunal to decide if the information is disclosed based on whether it will cause serious harm to the physical or mental health of the patient or others.

Even if a request to withhold part of the report is granted, reports will still be disclosed in full to the patient's solicitor or legal representative as long as they agree not to show them to the patient.

Sources and earlier reports

If information has come from a source other than personal experience, this source should be disclosed. If an earlier report is referred to, this report should also be attached.

INFORMATION FOR DETAINED PATIENTS

Hospitals and care homes have a legal duty to provide information to detained patients (Sections 132 and 133). This information includes:

- details of the section under which they are detained

- the powers of that section

- the patient's rights of appeal against that section

There is a statutory duty to ensure the above is done as soon as practicable after detention. The information must be provided both orally and in writing. The Code of Practice advises that the consultant (RMO), nurse or other professional giving the information be as helpful as possible and if it appears that the patient does not understand something, they should try and explain it further.

A list of the Patient Rights Leaflets for detained patients is given on page 122.

Additional information

There is also a duty to ensure that patients understand the following provisions of the Act and how they apply to them:

- the ways to be discharged from section
- restrictions on discharge by the nearest relative
- consent to treatment rules
- appeals to the Mental Health Review Tribunal
- the Code of Practice
- the role of the Mental Health Act Commission
- correspondence of patients

The nearest relative

The hospital must take practical steps (unless the patient requests otherwise) to give the nearest relative the same information as given to the patient. This should be done either when the patient is given the information or within a reasonable time afterwards.

Discharge

The person must be informed if they are discharged from detention or if the authority to detain them expires.

Unless the nearest relative has exercised their own powers of discharge (see page 92), the hospital must inform the nearest relative of any impending discharge of the patient. If practical, this information should be given at least seven days before the date of discharge. This duty is negated if either the patient or the nearest relative has stated that information regarding the patient's discharge should not be given to them.

Free legal representation

The patient should also be informed of the availability of free legal assistance for Mental Health Review Tribunal appeals.

The Act makes provision for the transfer of detained patients between different hospitals, across borders within the UK and outside of the UK. The rules relating to transfers differ based on the section a person is detained under. If a person is transferred under the Act, the power and responsibility to detain them is transferred to the new hospital.

Who can be transferred?

- People on short-term sections such as Sections 4, 5(2), 135(1) and 136 should not be transferred.
- People on longer term sections such as Sections 2, 3, 7 and 37 can be transferred by the hospital detaining them
- People on Court remand orders such as Sections 35, 36 and 38 would require permission from the Court involved
- People on forensic restricted sections such as Sections 37/41, 47/49 and 48/49 require the consent of the Home Office
- People under guardianship or supervised discharge can be transferred to other areas under the jurisdiction of a different local authority or NHS Trust

Transfers within a NHS Trust

The transfer of a person between different hospitals of the same NHS Trust is not classed as a transfer under the Act and so does not require any special procedures or paperwork. However, it should be noted that for Court remand orders (Sections 35, 36 and 38) or restricted sections (Section 37/41, 47/49 or 48/49) such moves should not be made without the prior permission of the Court or the Home Office respectively.

Note: Some restricted sections are made out to a specific named ward or unit and any movement of that person, even to another ward within the same building, would require the prior permission of the Home Office. In addition, even if a restricted section does not name a specific ward or unit, if the person is going to be moved to another ward in the same building with a lower level of security, permission from the Home Office is required.

Transfers within England and Wales

Detained patients transferring to different NHS Trusts within England and Wales require Form 24 to be completed by the sending hospital (together with the original section papers). These papers should go with the transferring patient and upon arrival the receiving hospital should complete the final part of the Form 24 which authorises them to detain the patient.

The transfer of any person remanded by a Court (Sections 35, 36 and 38) or under a restricted section (Section 37/41, 47/49 or 48/49) cannot be made without the prior permission of the Court or the Home Office respectively.

Transfers within UK borders

Transfers to Scotland, Northern Ireland, the Channel Islands or the Isle of Man require the additional intervention of either the Department of Health (for Section 2, 3 or 37) or the Home Office (for restricted sections). If they agree to the transfer they can authorise the continuous detention of the person across the English or Welsh border and allow for the conversion of the relevant section to the equivalent legislation in the receiving country.

If a person is being transferred into England or Wales from another part of the UK, the same process would apply. For example, the Scottish Department of Health would issue the authority, and on admission to hospital in England the receiving hospital would complete a Form 33.

Transfers outside the UK

The Act also provides the power to transfer a detained patient to countries outside the UK. This is used primarily to repatriate patients who do not have the right to live or remain in the UK. The power authorises the legal transfer of the patient (for example, in an aeroplane) to the receiving country. Once in the receiving country, it becomes that country's responsibility to apply their own legislation.

All such transfers require the prior consent of a Mental Health Review Tribunal hearing as well as authorisation by the Department of Health or the Home Office, depending on the section concerned.

Contact

Mental Health Programme
Department of Health, Wellington House, 133-155 Waterloo Road, London SE1 8UG
Tel: 020 7972 4548 Fax: 020 7972 4147

or

Mental Health Unit
The Home Office, 2nd Floor, Fry Building, 2 Marsham Street, London SW1P 4DF
Tel: 020 7035 1484 Fax: 020 7035 8974

Further information

The Mental Health Act Commission has produced a guidance note on the transfer of detained patients. For details visit *www.mhac.org.uk*.

Section 117 of the Act provides a legal right to after-care services for anyone who has been detained under the following sections of the legislation:

Sections 3, 37, 45A, 47 and 48

Once triggered, the right to after-care is ongoing and remains in place regardless of the person's circumstances. It only ends when both health and social services jointly agree that the person no longer requires after-care.

Responsibilities

Before a consultant (RMO) discharges a patient or grants them leave they should ensure that:

- ✓ the patient's health and social care needs have been assessed
- ✓ plans for those needs have been incorporated into their care plan
- ✓ the risks to the patient or others has been assessed
- ✓ if the patient is also an offender, the victim and their family have been considered

For those being discharged the consultant (RMO) should also consider:

- ✓ whether the patient meets the criteria for one of the Act's community sections supervised discharge (Section 25) or guardianship (Section 7)

Mental Health Review Tribunals and Hospital Managers' hearings

The Code of Practice advises that planning for after-care should be completed prior to a Mental Health Review Tribunal or Hospital Managers' hearing taking place.

The Care Programme Approach (CPA)

Section 117 of the Act contains the legal right to after-care, however it is through the CPA process that such after-care is assessed and delivered.

A patient's CPA should include:

- ➢ an assessment of their health and social care needs
- ➢ a care plan to provide for those needs
- ➢ a care co-ordinator to liaise with the patient and monitor their care
- ➢ the regular review of the care plan with changes made where necessary

Considerations for after-care

The following factors should be considered when a patient's aftercare is planned:

- ✓ patient's own wishes and needs
- ✓ wishes and needs of any dependants
- ✓ views of carers, relatives and friends
- ✓ patient's social and cultural background
- ✓ if the patient is an offender, the victim and their family should be taken into account when deciding where the patient should reside
- ✓ involving other organisations such as voluntary organisations
- ✓ a care co-ordinator to monitor the implementation of the care plan
- ✓ the identification of unmet needs

Assessment

In order to produce a comprehensive care plan the following areas should be assessed in order to identify any needs:

- employment and other activities
- accommodation
- out-patient treatment and counselling
- personal support
- assistance required in managing finances
- contingency plans in the event of a relapse

Once the patient's needs have been agreed, a timetable should be set to implement the various points of the care plan. The plan should be in writing and give details of the key people involved and their specific responsibilities.

After the plan is agreed, any proposed changes should be discussed with those involved in the care plan before they are implemented. The care co-ordinator is responsible for arranging regular reviews of the care plan.

Case Law

The Courts have ruled that a local authority has a mandatory duty to provide after-care under Section 117 and this after-care should not be subject to means testing. However, in providing after-care, the patient's financial position may be taken into account to establish their actual needs. For example, someone who already owned a house would not be prejudiced if local services did not provide them with housing. The Courts also accepted that funds are limited and services have to do the best they can with the resources available.

(From the case of: Tinsey (by his receiver and litigation friend Martin Conroy) v Sarker [2005] EWHC 192 (QB), February 2005)

Further information

Department of Health (1999) *Effective care co-ordination in mental health services: modernising the care programme approach – a policy booklet.*
Available from: *www.dh.gov.uk/PublicationsAndStatistics/Publications.*

The Mental Health Act Commission is the statutory body created by the Act to monitor the care and treatment of detained patients and also the wider operation of the legislation. It is made up of members (commissioners) with experience and knowledge of the Act. They include legal professionals, medical professionals, nurses, social workers and lay members. The Commission works under the direction of the Secretary of State for Health, however, it operates as an independent statutory body.

Contact

Mental Health Act Commission
Maid Marion House, 56 Hounds Gate, Nottingham NG1 6BG

Tel: 0115 943 7100   Fax: 0115 943 7101   Website: www.mhac.org.uk

Functions

The Commission performs the following functions:

> Appoints registered medical practitioners as second opinion approved doctors (SOADs) for the purposes of consent to treatment under the Act.

> Reviews the care and treatment of detained patients in hospitals or care homes. In order to do this the Commission or a person authorised by them may at any reasonable time:
> - visit and interview a patient
> - examine a patient in private (if they are a Commission appointed doctor)
> - ask to see a patient's records

> Reviews any decision to withhold post (Section 134) and may decide that the patient's post should not be withheld. The Commission's decision will be binding upon the hospital.

> Gives guidance on the practice and administration of the Act. A list of Commission guidance notes is given on page 123.

> Produces proposals for the update of the Code of Practice.

General protection of detained patients

The Commission carries out the following functions for the Secretary of State for Health as detailed in Section 120 of the Act in relation to detained patients. These include:

→ **Reviewing** – the use of the powers under the Act in relation to detained patients.

→ **Monitoring** – the operation of the consent to treatment provisions.

→ **Visiting** – and interviewing detained patients in hospitals and care homes.

→ **Investigating** – complaints by patients who are, or have been detained, under the Act (in relation to those periods of detention). Particularly complaints that the patient feels were not dealt with satisfactorily by the hospital or NHS Trust.

Working With The Mental Health Act 1983

→ **Investigating** – complaints made by Members of Parliament (MPs) regarding a detained patient. The Commission must inform the MP of the findings of any such investigation.

→ **Reporting** – the Commission produces biennial reports on its activities for the Secretary of State for Health and these are presented to Parliament. The most recent report covers the period 2003-2005 and is entitled *In Place of Fear?*

Investigation of complaints

Any person detained under the Act has the right to complain to the Commission about the period they were detained. The Commission may arrange to visit and interview the patient or they may ask the hospital to use the normal NHS complaints procedure and keep the Commission informed. Complaints can also be made by a patient's relative, friend or other person, providing it refers to a particular period of detention.

The Act excludes certain matters from investigation and does not bind an investigator of a complaint to continue where they do not feel it is appropriate to do so. For example, the Commission may consider it more appropriate for the complaint to be investigated by an alternative body such as the Parliamentary and Health Service Ombudsman.

Commission visits

The Commission undertakes regular visits to hospitals, care homes, high security hospitals and any other unit that houses people detained under the Act. Visiting commissioners may give notice of their visit, however, they are not under any obligation to do so and may visit without giving prior notice. It is an offence to refuse a commissioner access to patients or their records.

Death of detained patients

The Commission should be informed of the death of any patient detained under the Act. They will request full details of the circumstances and may send a commissioner to an inquest or other review.

Limitations

The Commission has no power to discharge a patient and can only visit and investigate issues relating to detained patients.

Future of the Commission

The government has agreed in principle that the Mental Health Act Commission as a stand alone body will end in April 2008 when it merges with both the Healthcare Commission and the Commission for Social Care Inspection.

A Code of Practice[10] and Memorandum[11] to the Act offer practical guidance on the application of the legislation. Both these documents should be read in conjunction with each other and the Mental Health Act 1983 itself. They can be downloaded from *www.markwalton.net.*

Legal status

The Act does not impose a legal duty to follow the Code of Practice, however failure to do so may be indicative of poor practice and be detrimental in the event of legal proceedings.

A recent Court judgment has confirmed the position of the Code of Practice as subservient to law. The case involved a complaint that Ashworth high security hospital was implementing seclusion procedures that did not follow the requirements of the Code of Practice.

The Court decided that Ashworth could take such action as it showed clear and cogent reasons for doing so. Consequently, hospitals may depart from the Code and develop their own policies and practices as long as they do not breach any rights under the European Convention on Human Rights. However, there should be 'cogent' reasons for any such departure from the Code's guidance.

(From the case of: R v Ashworth Hospital Authority (now Mersey Care National Health Service Trust) ex parte Munjaz [2005] UKHL 58)

Guiding principles

The Code of Practice begins by setting out the following guiding principles:

- ✓ Patients' human rights under the European Convention on Human Rights (ECHR) must be recognised.

- ✓ Patients' qualities, abilities and backgrounds must be respected.

- ✓ Account should be taken of a patient's age, gender, sexual orientation, social, ethnic, cultural and religious background and these elements must be respected, although they should not form the basis of assumptions.

- ✓ Patients' needs must be taken into account. However, the Code of Practice recognises there may be financial and practical restraints that make it difficult to meet these needs.

- ✓ Care or treatment should be provided in the least controlled and segregated facilities, provided that the safety of the patient and others is not compromised.

- ✓ Patients must be treated and cared for in a way that as much as possible promotes self-determination and personal responsibility consistent with their own needs and wishes.

- ✓ Patients must be discharged from detention or any other powers of the Act as soon as the powers or the detention are no longer needed.

Updates

The Code of Practice is periodically revised by the Mental Health Act Commission before going to the Secretary of State for Health and the Secretary of State for Wales. They then consult with appropriate groups on the changes before formally submitting the document to Parliament and the Welsh Assembly.

At the time of writing (September 2006) the most recent edition of the Code of Practice dates from 1999. A number of Court cases since then mean that several parts of the Code of Practice require revision. As a result the Mental Health Act Commission has produced a guidance note (see page 123) which gives updates to these parts. A fully revised version of the Code of Practice is expected once the proposed amendments to the legislation are agreed by Parliament. The Memorandum is in a similar position and was last published in 1998.

The Act gives specific legal powers to a detained patient's nearest relative. A nearest relative is not chosen or appointed by the patient in the same way as their next of kin, instead it is dictated by the legislation.

Hierarchy

The position of nearest relative is chosen in accordance with the hierarchy set out in Section 26 of the Act:

> **Husband or Wife**
> This includes people who have lived together as husband and wife for at least six months, including same-sex couples, as long as they are not married to someone else. If they are permanently separated, or one has deserted the other, they are excluded.

> **Son or Daughter**

> **Father or Mother**

> **Brother or Sister**
> The Act does not distinguish between half and full-blood relations so, a half-sister can be treated as a sister for the purposes of this section. However, where the patient has two sisters, one a full-blood sister and the other a half-sister the full-blood sister will take priority. The Act also gives the outdated explanation that an 'illegitimate child' will be treated as a legitimate child of their mother.

> **Grandparent**

> **Grandchild**

> **Uncle or Aunt**

> **Nephew or Niece**

For all of the above, if there is more than one person of equal standing in a category then the eldest one will be classed as the nearest relative.

Carers

If the patient was living with, and/or cared for by, any one of the relatives in the list above, that relative will be preferred as the nearest relative regardless of their position in the hierarchy. If there are two such relatives, the hierarchy will again take effect to decide which one of them will assume the position of nearest relative.

Excluded nearest relatives

The following people are excluded from being a nearest relative regardless of their position in the hierarchy:

- A non-resident of the UK, Channel Islands or the Isle of Man
- Anyone under 18 unless they are the husband/wife or father/mother of the patient
- Anyone with an (un-rescinded) order under Section 38 of the Sexual Offences Act 1956 which removes the relative's authority over the patient

Working With The Mental Health Act 1983

Detained patients who are not UK residents

Normally, if a relative is not resident in the UK they are excluded by the Act. However, if the patient is not a UK resident themselves (for example, a tourist or recent migrant) then the nearest relative may be a person not resident in the UK.

Unrelated nearest relative

A person who is unrelated to the patient may also be the nearest relative if they have lived with the patient for at least five years (but not as husband or wife). However, this person will be considered last in the hierarchy.

Nearest relative of a minor under guardianship

If a minor (someone under 18) is under guardianship or in the custody of a person, their nearest relative will be that person (to the exclusions of others) and not the relevant person in the hierarchy above.

The County Court's power to appoint a nearest relative

A County Court has the power to appoint another person to carry out the functions of the nearest relative if one of the following grounds apply:

> The patient has no nearest relative within the meaning of the Act or it is not reasonably practicable to find out if they have such a relative or who that relative is.

> The nearest relative is unable to act due to mental disorder or illness.

> The nearest relative of the person unreasonably objects to an application for Section 3 or guardianship.

> The nearest relative has exercised their power to discharge the person from hospital or guardianship without due regard to the person's welfare or the public interest.

Delegating authority of nearest relative

A nearest relative may authorise another person to perform their functions under the Act. The Memorandum to the Act states that the following rules apply in these circumstances:

- the authorised person does not have to be related to the person
- authorisation can be given at any time
- authorisation may be revoked at any time
- authorisation lapses on the death of the nearest relative giving it

While in force, such authorisation confers the functions of the nearest relative on the person authorised, to the exclusion of the person initially defined as nearest relative. The nearest relative should put their wishes in writing and the person nominated should confirm their acceptance in writing.

Rights

The nearest relative has the right to:

> ➤ receive written information about the patient's treatment (unless the patient objects).
> ➤ be consulted by and challenge decisions made by an approved social worker to use certain detention sections.
> ➤ be consulted on the making of a supervised discharge and on other key processes concerning this section.
> ➤ appeal to the Mental Health Review Tribunal on the patient's behalf (for some detention sections).
> ➤ attend a Mental Health Review Tribunal or Hospital Managers' hearing.
> ➤ be informed of the discharge of their relative.
> ➤ be informed if their relative is transferred to another hospital.
> ➤ request the local authority to assess their own needs if they provide a substantial amount of care under the Carers (Recognition and Services) Act 1995.

Powers

The nearest relative has the power to:

> ➤ delegate their powers to another person by putting this in writing.
> ➤ discharge the patient (for some detention sections).
> ➤ stop an application by an approved social worker for detention under Section 3 or guardianship. A Court would then be required to displace the relative in order to continue with the proposed detention.
> ➤ authorise a doctor to visit and examine the patient in order to advise on a decision to discharge the patient.
> ➤ apply for their relative to be assessed or treated under Section 2, 3 or 4 of the Act.

Power to discharge

One of the most significant powers given to a nearest relative is the power to discharge a patient under Section 2 or 3 of the Act. In order to exercise this power, they must inform the hospital in writing at least 72 hours before the intended discharge.

However, the exercise of this power is limited because it can be vetoed (stopped) by the consultant (RMO) if they believe that the patient, if discharged, is likely to act in a manner dangerous to themselves or others. This is done by the consultant completing Form 36 before the end of the 72 hour notice period required for such discharge.

The nearest relative also has the power to discharge a person from guardianship (Section 7). In this case the consultant has no power to prevent the discharge. However, depending on the circumstances, an application to displace the nearest relative could still be made.

Appeal against a consultant's objection

If discharge is blocked, the nearest relative may not exercise their powers of discharge for a further six months from the date of the consultant's Form 36.

However, the nearest relative may appeal against the consultant's veto to discharge by applying to the Mental Health Review Tribunal within 28 days. However, this only applies if the patient is detained under Section 3 of the Act.

Social services and the nearest relative

Approved social workers have a number of duties with regard to nearest relatives:

- ✓ Before an application under Section 2 is made, or within a reasonable time thereafter, the approved social worker must inform the nearest relative of the patient's detention and the nearest relative's power to discharge the patient.

- ✓ Before an application under Section 3 is made, the approved social worker must consult the nearest relative unless such consultation is not reasonably practicable or would involve unreasonable delay.

- ✓ If the nearest relative objects to a Section 3 or Section 7 application by an approved social worker, it cannot go ahead. However, the nearest relative may be displaced by a County Court where the objection is considered unreasonable.

- ✓ To make an assessment of the need to apply for the patient's detention in hospital if requested to do so by their nearest relative.

Case Law

A recent case has examined the circumstances under which an approved social worker must consult and/or inform a nearest relative. The decision in this case means that the advice given in paragraph 2.16 of the Code of Practice is now incorrect. The local authority (social services) had felt that to comply with the Act, they could not give an undertaking to E that they would not consult or inform her nearest relative when they were assessing her for detention under Section 2 or 3 of the Act.

The Court decided this was wrong and stated that the term 'practicability of consulting' the nearest relative is actually a balancing exercise between not only the availability of the nearest relative but also the patient's rights, in particular, their right to respect for private and family life.

The main considerations in this judgment were that the patient had expressed the view that her nearest relative should not be involved, the fact that the nearest relative herself did not wish to be involved and the likelihood that involvement would have been distressing for the patient. The psychiatrist had also said that E's mental health could be damaged if she knew that her sister would be consulted against her wishes.

(From the case of: R (on the application of E) v Bristol City Council [2005] EWHC 74 (Admin) 23rd February 2006)

Amending the Act

The government plans to amend part of the Act in relation to nearest relatives. This will include changing the powers for the displacement of relatives and recognising Civil Partnerships (see page 97).

Further information

The Mental Health Act Commission has produced two guidance notes on nearest relatives (see page 123).

Section 127 of the Act contains a criminal offence for the ill-treatment or wilful neglect of people who have a mental disorder. It is punishable by a maximum of two years imprisonment.

Legal criteria

• Any employee of a hospital or care home who ill-treats or wilfully neglects a mentally disordered in-patient or out-patient on the premises of the hospital or care home.

In addition it also extends to:

• any individual who is a guardian or otherwise caring for a mentally disordered person under the Act who ill-treats or wilfully neglects the person in their care.

• any individual who ill-treats or wilfully neglects a person with mental disorder they are caring for. This can be on any premises and applies even if the person is not detained under the Act.

There is no requirement for the mental disorder to be diagnosed or for the person to have received treatment, they can simply appear to suffer from a mental disorder.

Case Law

A single act can be enough to satisfy the criteria of this section. In this case a slap to the patient's face.

(From the case of: R v Holmes [1979] Crim. L. R. 52, Bodmin Crown Court)

Other offences

The Act also contains a number of other criminal offences:

- committing forgery (Section 126)
- making false statements (Section 126)
- assisting patients to go absent without leave (Section 128)
- obstruction (Section 129)

Bringing proceedings

It is standard in criminal matters for the Director of Public Prosecutions to institute proceedings. However, with this offence a local authority (social services) may also institute proceedings although in some circumstances they may need the consent of the Director of Public Prosecutions.

The Mental Capacity Act 2005

An offence of ill-treatment or neglect is also contained in the Mental Capacity Act 2005 in relation to people lacking capacity. It has a longer maximum prison term of up to five years attached to it.

Sexual Offences Act 2003

This legislation contains a series of offences designed to protect people with mental health problems from sexually abusive acts by others including care workers.

In March 2006 the government announced its intention to amend some parts of the Act[8]. However, these amendments will leave most of the 1983 legislation unchanged and it is also likely to be several years before they come into effect. At the time of writing (September 2006) the amendments are as follows:

Supervised community treatment

A new community section similar to supervised discharge (Section 25), but with an additional power that if a person refuses treatment in the community they can be recalled to hospital for compulsory treatment. The section would also include a power to recall and detain the person in hospital without having to complete a full Section 3.

Definition of mental disorder

The definition of mental disorder will be simplified and the four categories of disorder (mental illness, mental impairment, severe mental impairment and psychopathic disorder) will be abolished. This means that some people who are excluded from the Act at present may come under the remit of the legislation in the future, for example people with acquired brain injuries. A limitation will apply to people with learning disabilities (as at present) such that the learning disability will only be treated as a mental disorder under the Act if associated with abnormally aggressive or seriously irresponsible conduct.

The present exclusions relating to promiscuity, immoral conduct and sexual deviancy are to be removed. This is not designed to change the current position, but rather to recognise that they are behavioural descriptions and not mental disorders.

The current exclusion relating to dependence on alcohol or drugs is to be re-worded. Whilst a dependence on alcohol or drugs is not a mental disorder and so is excluded from the legislation, a person may be dependent on drugs or alcohol and also have a mental disorder which would come under the remit of the Act. The change of wording aims to clarify this.

Criteria for detention

Appropriate treatment is to be included in the legal criteria for Sections 2 and 3. The intention is to tighten the criteria for detention to encourage mental health services to make a holistic assessment as to whether appropriate treatment is available before detaining someone.

The *treatability test,* one of the current criteria for several of the long-term sections (Sections 3, 37 and 47), is to be abolished. At present the criterion states that to detain a person with psychopathic disorder or mental impairment, the treatment is "likely to alleviate or prevent a deterioration of the condition". This will be removed as a criterion for detention under the Act, for the renewal of the section and also as a consideration for discharge by the Mental Health Review Tribunal.

Nearest relative

A new power for patients to apply to the County Court to change (displace) their nearest relative as identified in the hierarchy of relatives given in the Act. This would be granted if the relative was too ill to act, was using their powers unreasonably or if it was "reasonable that the person should not act as the relative".

Civil partners (Civil Partnership Act 2005) will be formally recognised in the Mental Health Act as equivalent to spouses in the nearest relative hierarchy.

Professional roles

Approved Mental Health Professionals will replace approved social workers *(ASWs)*

Their role will remain the same, but professionals other than social workers will be able to qualify, for example community psychiatric nurses and occupational therapists. As with the current ASW system a person would have to undertake specific training to become approved. Local authorities (social services) will be responsible for approving staff, however the person will not have to be a local authority employee.

Clinical Supervisors will replace responsible medical officers (RMOs)

Their role will remain the same but professionals other than consultant psychiatrists will be able to qualify, for example psychologists, nurses and social workers. All clinical supervisors will have to undertake a training course which will cover their key responsibilities including granting leave of absence, discharge of sections, renewal of sections and consent to treatment procedures.

Bournewood Gap

This amendment applies to the Mental Capacity Act 2005 but is being introduced with the above amendments as it is intended that they all go before Parliament together. It aims to resolve the issue of the Bournewood Gap that is the admission and treatment of people who lack capacity, placed in an environment (a ward or care home) that amounts to detention (deprivation of liberty). The amendment will allow a means of detaining people who lack capacity. For more information see *The Bournewood Judgement* on page 100.

Mental Health Review Tribunal

The amendments will increase the speed and frequency of Mental Health Review Tribunals for certain patients detained under the Act. This will be done by:

- reducing the time taken to arrange Tribunals
- giving patients who are detained for long periods more frequent Tribunals
- reducing the time allowed before staff must refer patients who have not appealed to the Tribunal at all or for a considerable period of time

Further information

For further details contact:

Mental Health Bill Policy Team
Tel: 020 7972 4477
Email: MentalHealthBill@dh.gsi.gov.uk
Website: www.dh.gov.uk/mentalhealth

VOLUNTARY (INFORMAL) PATIENTS

At any given time approximately 62% of people on mental health wards are informal (voluntary) patients[2]. Section 131 of the Mental Health Act states that although the legislation can be used to detain and treat people against their will, it does not have to be used at all and any person can admit themselves voluntarily and stay in hospital as an informal patient.

Rights of informal patients

If a patient is in hospital informally and therefore not detained under the Act, no restrictions may be placed upon that patient.

Informal patients have the following legal rights:

- ✓ They must be free to come and go as they please and without restriction.

- ✓ They cannot be forcibly medicated (unless under *Common Law Powers*, page 102).

- ✓ They can discharge themselves at any time.

- ✓ They can agree to a care plan (or 'contract') but they are not bound by it.

The Code of Practice states that informal patients should be told by staff that they may leave at any time.

However, if an informal patient wishes to discharge themselves against the judgment of the mental health team, they may be assessed and if they meet the criteria of the Act they could then be detained.

Working With The Mental Health Act 1983

THE BOURNEWOOD JUDGMENT

The Bournewood judgment (*the case of HL v the United Kingdom (Application no. 4508/99) decision of 5th October 2004*) set a legal precedent. The case clearly stated that if a person, who lacks capacity to agree to their admission and stay on a ward (or a care home), is kept in an environment that deprives them of their liberty, they cannot be classed as a voluntary/informal patient. This is because there is no legal basis for their effective detention and consequently no legal right of appeal.

The facts

- HL was an adult male who suffered from autism.

- HL lacked the capacity to either consent or object to medical treatment.

- HL was at a day care centre when he became unwell. The hospital responsible for his care and treatment was contacted.

- The hospital considered admitting HL under the Mental Health Act but decided that since HL showed no intention of leaving he could be admitted as an informal patient.

- The approach taken by the hospital complied with the Code of Practice to the Mental Health Act 1983 which states that if at the time of admission a patient lacks capacity to consent, but does not object to entering hospital and receiving care or treatment, the admission should be informal.

However, HL complained that the time he spent in hospital as an informal patient amounted to a deprivation of liberty and that this was neither in accordance with a procedure prescribed by law or lawful, under the terms of the European Convention on Human Rights.

HL further argued that the procedures available to him to review the legality of his detention did not satisfy the requirements of the Convention.

The judgment

The European Court of Human Rights stated that there had been a violation of Article 5(1)e because there had been a lack of effective procedure to determine the admission and detention of HL, who lacked capacity but was compliant.

The Court found that the conditions under which HL was kept meant he was deprived of his liberty and therefore effectively detained but with no legal process being applied. The Court noted the following factors as evidence of HL's deprivation of liberty:

The healthcare professionals exercised complete and effective control over HL's:

➢ Assessment

➢ Care

➢ Treatment

➢ Contacts

➢ Movement

➢ Residence

He was under constant supervision and control and was not free to leave.

Resolution of the Bournewood Judgment

In response to the Bournewood judgment, the government has announced plans to amend the Mental Capacity Act 2005 to permit the detention of people who lack capacity in circumstances covered by the Bournewood judgment (see page 97).

However, it remains a matter of legal debate as to what exactly are the key conditions that have to be met in order to constitute an environment that deprives a person of their liberty. The Court gave some guidance but it is open to interpretation. The fact that in the Bournewood case the carers/relatives wanted the person discharged and this was refused does not mean it is the central criteria to be met for the Bournewood conditions to be triggered. It will probably be for future Court judgments to provide a more precise definition. For example, would a care home that allowed a resident (who lacked capacity) to go out, but only if they were escorted, be a detaining environment? Or does the judgment require a combination of several factors working together?

In addition to the powers of the Mental Health Act, there are also powers of detention and treatment under common law. However, these powers generally only apply to patients who lack capacity. Common law is essentially case law as opposed to statute law and is defined by a series of cases that have gone before the Courts resulting in judgments. These judgments lead to legal principles being set. As statute law the Mental Health Act gives staff considerable legal protection for the actions they take. The same cannot be said for common law. If common law is used by staff in place of the Act, the Courts would expect to see clear evidence of a situation that meant the powers of the Mental Health Act could not be used and the reasons for this.

Consent and patients with capacity

It should be remembered that every adult with capacity has a basic right to refuse medical treatment even if that refusal could cause permanent injury to health or premature death. However, where a person is found to lack capacity, their inability to consent to medical treatment may be overridden under common law.

Emergency treatment for patients who lack capacity

If a medical emergency arises and a person lacks capacity suddenly (for example because they have lost consciousness), medical treatment may still be provided. The treatment must be assessed as being in the person's best interests.

It is for the doctor treating the patient to decide whether a proposed treatment is in their best interests. However, if a dispute is taken to Court, a judge will decide whether that treatment was indeed in the patient's best interests. Reasonable force may be used to ensure that a patient lacking capacity may be treated.

Restraint under the common law doctrine of necessity

Staff may use powers under common law to prevent a voluntary (informal) patient from causing *immediate* harm to themselves or others. This is not a long-term power and should end once the criteria are no longer met or, where appropriate, the Mental Health Act can be applied.

Mental Capacity Act 2005

From April 2007, the treatment and restraint of people lacking capacity will be covered by the Mental Capacity Act 2005 (see page 103).

The Mental Capacity Act 2005 provides powers to enable health, social care and financial decisions to be made on behalf of a person who lacks capacity. The Act will place a positive duty upon anyone making decisions on someone else's behalf to ensure that they have properly assessed that person's capacity. Any decisions made in a person's best interests must be in accordance with this legislation. The legislation will come into force in April 2007.

Facts

The annual census of in-patients in mental health units for 2005 indicates that on any one day, there are at least 6,000 people who are informal (voluntary) patients who lack capacity to consent to treatment[2] or to make other health and social care decisions. Every one of these patients will come under the auspices of the Mental Capacity Act 2005 and require a formal assessment of their capacity and further action under this Act if treatment and care is to be given legally.

Principles

The Act begins with five statutory principles. These must be followed whenever the Mental Capacity Act is used. They are:

1. **An assumption of capacity**
   A person must always be assumed to have capacity unless it is proven otherwise. The Act provides a standard test to assess a person's capacity.

2. **All practicable steps to assist**
   Someone cannot be judged as lacking capacity until all practicable steps have been taken to assist them make a decision without success.

3. **Unwise decisions**
   An unwise decision does not in itself mean a person lacks capacity.

4. **Best interests**
   Any decision made, or any act undertaken, on behalf of a person lacking capacity, must be in the person's best interests. The legislation provides a statutory checklist which must be used to decide what is in a person's best interests.

5. **Least restrictive option**
   Before any decision is made, or any act is undertaken, on behalf of a person lacking capacity, the least restrictive options available in terms of the person's rights and freedoms should be considered.

Key duties and powers

The Act provides the following key duties and powers in relation to those lacking capacity:

- ✓ definition of capacity
- ✓ test for assessing capacity
- ✓ checklist for making decisions on behalf of others
- ✓ power to undertake acts on behalf of people regarding their care and treatment
- ✓ criteria for restraint
- ✓ procedures for making payments on behalf of others

Working With The Mental Health Act 1983

103

The Act creates specific legal routes to give others decision-making powers on behalf of someone who lacks capacity. These are:

✓ Deputyship (replacing receivership)
✓ Lasting powers of attorney (replacing enduring powers of attorney)

The legislation also allows someone with capacity to state their wishes concerning future treatment through an 'advance decision' which would become effective should they lose the capacity to make decisions in the future.

Court of Protection

Until recently, matters of health and social care relating to those who lacked capacity were taken to the High Court. Matters regarding finance and property were decided in the Court of Protection. However, when in force, the Mental Capacity Act will bring together these four areas to be dealt with by a new Court of Protection:

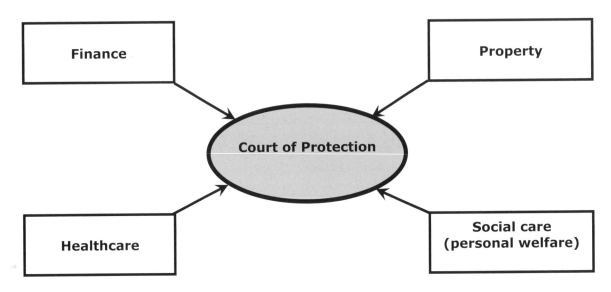

Interaction with the Mental Health Act 1983

A person may be affected by both the Mental Health Act 1983 and the Mental Capacity Act 2005 simultaneously. The most likely groups of people are those with a severe learning disability or dementia who are detained in hospital under the Mental Health Act. If decisions about treatment (not for mental disorder) are required and the person lacks capacity the Mental Capacity Act could be used. However, the Mental Health Act will override the Mental Capacity Act on decisions concerning treatment for mental disorder.

It should be stressed that the two Acts are totally independent of each other in their application. A mental disorder does not mean a person lacks capacity and a lack of capacity does not necessarily mean that a person is mentally unwell. Further, a determination of capacity can only be made once an assessment has been completed under the Mental Capacity Act, not through any other form of testing.

Part VII of the Mental Health Act 1983 will be repealed with the implementation of the Mental Capacity Act 2005. This Part governs financial powers in relation to people who lack capacity and the appointment of receivers. They will be replaced by deputies appointed by the Court of Protection.

Differences between the two Acts

	Mental Health Act 1983	Mental Capacity Act 2005
Purpose	The detention and treatment of people with mental disorder.	The assessment of capacity and the power to make health and social care decisions on behalf of people lacking capacity. The power to make financial decisions for people lacking capacity is also included.
Client group	Only people with mental disorder.	Any person with reduced capacity, including people with dementia, learning disability, mental disorder, brain injury and autism.
Location	Primarily limited to hospitals or other registered settings.	Anywhere that a decision needs to be made, for example in the home, in hospital, or a GP surgery.
Treatment	Treatment for mental disorder only.	Any health or social care intervention.
Staff	Use of the Act is limited to specific professionals and these are primarily from mental health services. A nearest relative also has certain powers.	Any staff group providing health or social care interventions for people who lack capacity including professional staff and those from care homes and voluntary agencies. Relatives and carers can also use the Act.

Which Act to use?

The question of which Act to use, if a person lacks capacity and has a mental disorder, is left to the professional judgment of those involved:

> ➤ If the mental disorder requires treatment, the Mental Capacity Act could be used for treatment, provided the person is not already detained under a section of the Mental Health Act which allows treatment against a person's consent.

> ➤ Both Acts could apply to a person at the same time. For example, someone detained under Section 136 of the Mental Health Act 1983 (which does not include the power to treat a person without their consent) could be treated for mental disorder under the powers of the Mental Capacity Act 2005 if they lacked capacity.

> ➤ If a person detained under any section of the Mental Health Act required treatment not related to their mental disorder, they could be treated under the powers of the Mental Capacity Act.

The draft Code of Practice to the Mental Capacity Act has given the following as examples of when the Mental Health Act 1983 would be used in place of the Mental Capacity Act 2005:

- **Advance decision to refuse treatment for mental disorder**
  In this instance, the treatment could not be lawfully provided under the Mental Capacity Act 2005 and consequently the Mental Health Act would have to be used instead. However, any objections in the advance decision should be noted as if they were being made by the person at that time.

Working With The Mental Health Act 1983

- **Detention is necessary**

  If the only practical way to treat a person is by detaining them and depriving them of their liberty the Mental Health Act would be more appropriate.

- **Constant resistance to treatment**

  Where possible, it would be better to use the Mental Health Act where there is constant or repeated resistance to treatment.

- **Risk**

  If it appears that harm may come to the person or someone else because they cannot receive necessary treatment under the Mental Capacity Act, it would be more appropriate to use the Mental Health Act 1983.

Policies affected

The introduction of the Mental Capacity Act in April 2007 will require mental health NHS Trusts and other organisations to amend a number of their policies and introduce new ones to ensure compliance with the legislation. Some examples are given below:

➢ *Access to records*

Under the Act if an independent mental capacity advocate (IMCA) is appointed for someone who lacks capacity the advocate has a legal right to view and copy NHS, local authority and care home records relating to their client and the issue for which they have been referred. This places a legal duty on the record holder to provide the information and does not require the consent of the patient concerned.

➢ *Care Programme Approach (CPA)*

The role and authority of both independent mental capacity advocates and lasting powers of attorney will need to be incorporated into CPA policies. An advocate under the Act may need to attend CPA meetings on behalf of their client and make a submission as to what they consider is in the patient's best interests. A lasting power of attorney with the appropriate authority will be the only person who can consent to health and social care decisions on behalf of a person lacking capacity and will therefore need to attend such meetings.

➢ *Restraint*

The Act provides the power to restraint a person lacking capacity. NHS Trusts with existing policies on restraint will have to incorporate this new power and consider the guidance it gives to staff in relation to its use.

➢ *Consent to treatment*

The Act fundamentally provides a means to assess a person's capacity to consent to health and social care interventions. Any existing policy on obtaining consent from patients will need to incorporate the new legislation.

In addition if a patient has a lasting power of attorney under the Act in relation to healthcare decisions then the attorney will decide whether or not to consent to treatment on behalf of the patient if they lack capacity. The doctor does not have the authority to make treatment decisions in this case rather they will give their clinical recommendations for treatment to the lasting power of attorney who will make the decision. The exception to this is if the patient is detained under the Mental Health Act 1983 and the treatment is for mental disorder.

➢ *Advance decisions*

Organisations should already have policies on the use of advance directives. The new Act provides statutory rules governing the authority and procedure for making advance decisions. Policies will need to incorporate these rules and also clarify for staff the authority of the Mental Health Act over advance decisions.

> *Vulnerable adults*

The Act provides a number of mechanisms that can be used to take action for people who lack capacity and for whom vulnerable adult procedures are being initiated. For example, it introduces a new power via the Court of Protection to limit or prevent the contact a vulnerable person has with an abuser.

> *Advocacy*

Organisations are placed under a legal duty to refer certain patients to independent mental capacity advocates (for example a person lacking capacity to consent to admission to a care home where the NHS is funding the placement under continuing care arrangements and the person has no relatives or others to consult). There will need to be referral procedures in place to ensure they are compliant with the new legislation.

> *Mental Health Act 1983*

The Mental Health Act and Mental Capacity Act overlap in a number of areas and policies will need to be updated. If a patient who lacks capacity is detained under the Mental Health Act and has a lasting power of attorney (with the appropriate authority), the attorney will effectively assume the role of the patient and be able to exercise the patient's rights, for example they can appeal to the Mental Health Review Tribunal (if the section the patient is detained under allows such an appeal).

Further information

It is not within the scope of this guide to go into further detail on the Mental Capacity Act 2005. For a more detailed guide to this legislation, see *Working With The Mental Capacity Act 2005* also published by Matrix Training Associates.

Matrix Training Associates
2 The Green, North Waltham, Hampshire RG25 2BQ
Tel: 01256 398 928
Fax: 01256 398 929
Email: books@matrixtrainingassociates.com
Website: www.matrixtrainingassociates.com

Further information on the Act can also be obtained from:

Mental Capacity Implementation Programme
Department of Constitutional Affairs, Steel House, 11 Tothill Street, London SW1H 9LH
Tel: 020 7210 0037
Fax: 020 7210 0007
Email: makingdecisions@dca.gsi.gov.uk
Website: www.dca.gov.uk/mencap/index.htm

Section 47 of the National Assistance Act 1948 provides for the compulsory admission of a person to a hospital or care home who may not necessarily have a mental illness or disorder but need assistance in looking after themselves.

Section 47 criteria

An application may be made to a Magistrates' Court by the local authority (social services) on the following grounds:

The person is suffering from a grave chronic disease

or

the person is elderly or physically incapacitated and is living in insanitary conditions and they are unable to look after themselves or are not being given proper care and attention by others

and

it is necessary to remove the person from their place of residence either in their own interests or to prevent injury or serious nuisance to others.

A doctor must make a written report or give oral evidence to the Court confirming the criteria above.

Limitations and duration

➤ Although the National Assistance Act allows admission, it does not permit treatment to be given to a person without their consent.

➤ The initial period of detention is three months, which can be extended by further orders of the Court.

➤ After six weeks has passed from the start of the order under Section 47, the person subject to the order (or someone on their behalf) may apply to the Court to end it.

Working With The Mental Health Act 1983

In general the Act does not have a minimum age limit except in relation to guardianship and supervised discharge where the minimum age is 16.

If it is necessary to admit and/or treat a child or young person in hospital, the local authority (social services) and the NHS should ensure they are familiar with both the Mental Health Act 1983 and the Children Act 1989.

Facts

Figures show that during the nine months from 1st January to 30th September 2003 over 250 children (under the age of 18) were detained under the Mental Health Act on adult mental health wards[12]. This figure does not include children also detained in specialist child and adolescent units.

Guiding principles

The Code of Practice sets out the following special considerations for children:

- ✓ children should be kept informed about their care and treatment
- ✓ children's views and wishes should be sought and considered
- ✓ the impact of their wishes on their parents (or those with parental responsibility) should also be considered
- ✓ intervention due to mental disorder should be the least restrictive option possible
- ✓ children should have the least possible segregation from their family, friends, community and school
- ✓ appropriate education should be given to all children in hospital

Mental Health Act 1983 v Children Act 1989

When dealing with young persons under the age of 18, the suitability of the Children Act as opposed to the Mental Health Act should be considered. The child's needs should be assessed and if the key issue is mental health treatment then the Mental Health Act should be used. However, if the child's behaviour is the central factor, then the Children Act may be more appropriate. The legislation providing the best consistency in the child's care and the least restrictive option to achieve the care and treatment objectives should be chosen.

Children under 16: care and treatment

The Code of Practice states that the following questions should be answered when considering the care and treatment of a child under 16:

- ➤ who has parental responsibility?
- ➤ if the child's parents are separated, is there a residence order?
- ➤ has the child's capacity been assessed?
- ➤ is the refusal to consent to treatment by a parent, or a person with parental responsibility, reasonable?
- ➤ could the child's needs be met through an alternative method, for example a social services or educational placement? Have the alternatives been properly considered?

Fraser guidelines (known previously as Gillick competence)

Under the Fraser guidelines a child (under 16) is considered competent if:

- ✓ they have the capacity to make a decision about the proposed treatment
  and
- ✓ they have sufficient understanding and intelligence to be capable of making up their own mind.

This definition was established in the case of *Gillick v West Norfolk and Wisbech Area Health Authority and Another* [1986] AC and further developed by the case of Re: R [1992] 1 FLR 190. Note: Although commonly referred to as *Gillick competence*, Mrs Gillick, who initiated the proceedings, does not wish her name to be associated with the case and it is now named after the judge in the case, Lord Fraser.

Informal admission to hospital

Children under 16

A parent, or a person with parental responsibility, may consent on behalf of a child under 16 to admission to hospital. This may also be the case even if the child is established as being competent (Fraser guidelines) and they do not want to be admitted. Similarly, a competent child's wish to discharge themselves can be overridden by a parent or a person with parental responsibility.

In contrast, if a competent child agrees to admission but a parent or a person with parental responsibility opposes the admission, although their opposing view will be given consideration and due weight, it will not necessarily take precedence over the child's view.

Children aged 16 or 17

A 16 or 17 year old able to express their own wishes, can admit themselves to hospital as an informal patient. If they cannot express their own wishes, parental consent should be sought or detention under the Mental Health Act considered.

Consent to treatment

Children under 18

If the child is established as being competent they can give valid consent to treatment. If they are assessed as lacking capacity (and therefore not competent) then consent may be sought from a parent or a person with parental responsibility. Refusal of treatment by a competent child can be overridden by the Courts, a parent or a person with parental responsibility.

Children looked after by social services

If children are looked after by social services, treatment decisions should be discussed with a parent or a person with parental responsibility.

Children voluntarily accommodated by social services

If treatment is proposed, the consent of a parent or a person with parental responsibility must be obtained.

Children subject to a care order

In this situation, parental responsibility is shared between the parents and social services and consequently, it is a matter to be agreed between the two parties. Social services have power under the Children Act to limit parental responsibility if needed.

Placement of children

It is preferable to place children with others in their own age group. In exceptional circumstances, the Code of Practice states that 'discreet accommodation' in a ward with adults which has appropriate staffing and facilities in respect of the child may also be acceptable.

When should you go to Court?

The Code of Practice gives examples of when a Court's decision-making powers may need to be sought:

1. If treatment decisions need to be made in relation to a child who does not meet the Fraser guidelines
   and
   the person with parental responsibility cannot be identified
   or
   the person with parental responsibility is incapacitated.

2. If the person with parental responsibility does not appear to be acting in the best interests of the child when making treatment decisions for them.

When making decisions for a child, weight should be given to the child's refusal to be treated in proportion with their age and maturity.

Further information

The care and treatment of children is a complex area and further reading is recommended. The Mental Health Act Commission has produced a guidance note on detaining children (see page 123). Further information about the Fraser guidelines is available via: *www.dh.gov.uk* (search under *consent*).

VOTING

The Representation of the People Act 2000 allowed the use of a psychiatric hospital address for the purposes of registering to vote. This has enabled both voluntary (informal) patients and some detained patients to vote.

In order to register to vote, patients can use any of the following addresses:

- ✓ their own address
- ✓ an address to which they have a local connection
- ✓ the address at which they are an in-patient

If the person is a voluntary patient but unable to leave the ward to vote in person, they can arrange to vote by proxy or make an application for postal voting. A detained patient can only vote by proxy or by post.

Exception

People detained under a forensic (Court or prison) section of the Act cannot vote.

Further information

The Mental Health Act Commission has produced a guidance note on voting (see page 123).

Section 134 of the Act allows hospitals to withhold post sent by or to detained patients in certain circumstances. There are detailed procedures that apply in the event of post being withheld and any decision to do so may be subject to review by the Mental Health Act Commission.

Legal criteria

A patient's out-going post may be withheld if:

it is addressed to a person who has stated they no longer wish
to receive post from the patient

or

the patient is at a high security hospital **and** it is considered that the post
is likely to cause distress to the addressee or to any other person
(this does not apply to members of hospital staff)

or

the patient is at a high security hospital **and** the post is likely
to cause danger to any person.

Likewise, in-coming post can be withheld from a patient detained in a high security hospital if it is considered to be in the interests of the patient's safety or for the protection of others.

Application

A person can make a request to have post withheld from them by writing to either the hospital, the consultant (RMO) in charge of the patient's treatment or the Secretary of State for Health.

Exceptions

Some organisations and persons are exempt from the above rules. That is, post can neither be stopped going to them or being delivered from them. They include:

➢ Members of Parliament (House of Commons and House of Lords)
➢ Masters (Judges) or any other officers of the Court of Protection
➢ The Parliamentary and Health Service Ombudsman
➢ Mental Health Review Tribunal
➢ NHS organisations (Primary Care Trust, Strategic Health Authority)
➢ Local authorities (social services)
➢ A legal representative of the patient
➢ Independent advocacy organisations

Inspection and record keeping

Full details on the procedure for inspecting and retaining post are given in the Memorandum to the Act available on *www.markwalton.net*.

At the time of writing (September 2006) there are three different ways of managing the finances of people who lack the capacity to do so themselves:

- Receivership and the Court of Protection (Mental Health Act 1983)
- Enduring powers of attorney (Enduring Powers of Attorney Act 1985)
- Appointeeship (Social Security (Claims and Payments) Regulations 1987)

From April 2007, the Mental Capacity Act will come into force and replace both receivership and enduring powers of attorney.

Receivership

The Court of Protection may appoint a receiver to undertake the management of the property and/or finances of someone who lacks capacity. The Court can also make a one-off judgment to release money or another asset. If the person's income is solely from state benefits then appointeeship can be used instead.

The Court of Protection has specific powers in relation to a person's property and affairs including:

- ❑ control and management of the patient's property (including its sale)
- ❑ allowing someone else to carry out a contract which was originally entered into by the person
- ❑ dissolving a partnership of which the person was a member
- ❑ conducting legal proceedings in the name of the person or on their behalf

The Mental Capacity Act replaces receivership with a new system of Court appointed deputies. In essence, the role will be the same in relation to finance and property. However, deputies may also be given the power to manage health and social care decisions. These additional powers will not be granted automatically but will be at the discretion of the Court taking into account the individual circumstances of each case.

Enduring powers of attorney

A person may plan ahead and appoint someone to act as their attorney to deal with their finances and property in the event that they are unable to do so themselves at some point in the future. Once a person loses capacity, the attorney (the person exercising the power) must register the enduring power of attorney with the Court of Protection.

The Mental Capacity Act replaces enduring powers of attorney with a new system called lasting powers of attorney. The new power of attorney will be able to manage not only financial affairs but also health and social care decisions on behalf of a person who lacks capacity.

Appointeeship

An appointee is someone authorised by the benefits agency to receive and manage state benefits, such as income support or a pension, on behalf of a person who lacks capacity to manage their finances. The Mental Capacity Act will not affect the system of appointeeship.

The Data Protection Act 1998

The Data Protection Act 1998 gives patients the right to view and/or copy information held about them. It supersedes the previous right of access under the Access to Health Records Act 1990. The right to access extends to patients detained under the Mental Health Act 1983.

Applications to access records

Following a verbal or written request to view or obtain copies of their medical records, patients may be given a photocopy or computer printout of their records. There is no legal requirement to make a formal application and the Data Protection Act does not prevent a doctor from allowing patients access to their records informally as long as no other provisions of the Data Protection Act are breached.

Access extends to all manual and computerised health records and there is no limit to access depending on the age of the records.

Applicants

Patients may apply for access to their own records, or authorise a third party to access them on their behalf. Parents can access their child's records if it is in the child's best interests but this may be opposed by a competent child. Receivers may also apply for access.

Restrictions

Information likely to cause serious physical or mental harm to the patient or another person can be withheld. The same applies to information given by a third party who has not consented to the disclosure of that information (unless the third party in question is a health professional who has cared for the patient).

Fees for Access to Records

To provide access and copies:

Computer records	£10
Manual records	£50 (maximum)
Computer and manual records	£50 (maximum)

To provide access to read records only:

Computer records	£10
Manual records	£10
Computer and manual records	£10

In relation to access to read manual records, if the records have been added to in the last 40 days, no charge can be made.

Time limits

Prompt access should be given and must be given within 40 days of the receipt of the request and fee.

The following case studies give examples of the Act in practice.

Case study 1: General application of the Act

Julie is in a supermarket when she starts to suffer delusions and because of her behaviour the police are called. PC Nancoo arrives and tries to calm Julie down but, by her demeanour, suspects that she may be suffering from a mental disorder. PC Nancoo assesses that Julie needs immediate care or control and for the protection of herself or others needs to remove her to a place of safety.

In this situation the following process could be instigated under the Act:

> ➢ PC Nancoo's assessment of the situation means that she has the power to take Julie to a place of safety (hospital in this case) for assessment (Section 136).
> ➢ Julie arrives at hospital and is assessed the following day. Two doctors (one of them Section 12 approved) and an approved social worker assess Julie and she is detained under Section 2. Section 2 is considered appropriate to detain Julie for assessment under the Act because this is her first encounter with mental health services.
> ➢ After three weeks under Section 2, it is concluded that Julie has a *mental illness of a nature or degree that requires treatment in hospital for her own safety.* Following another assessment by two doctors (one Section 12 approved) and an approved social worker, Julie is detained under Section 3.
> ➢ Whilst on Section 3, Julie decides to appeal against her detention and makes an appeal to the Mental Health Review Tribunal. The hearing takes six weeks to arrange and Julie is unsuccessful as the Tribunal is not satisfied that she meets the criteria for discharge.
> ➢ Three weeks later Julie wishes to appeal again and contacts her solicitor who advises her that as she has already appealed to the Tribunal during this period of detention (the first six months of a Section 3) she cannot do so again. However, he also advises her that she has a right of appeal to the Hospital Managers. Julie instructs her solicitor to appeal on her behalf.
> ➢ At the Hospital Managers' hearing, three weeks later, Julie is discharged.

Case study 2: Appeals and discharge criteria

Sarah is detained under Section 3 of the Act and decides to appeal to the Mental Health Review Tribunal. She has appealed once already to the Tribunal in her last period of detention. However, she is able to appeal to the Tribunal again now her Section 3 has been extended (renewed) for a second six month period.

The medical and social work reports for the Tribunal are, on the whole, positive about Sarah's condition. During the Tribunal hearing her solicitor, Mr James, establishes that although she has a mental illness it is not of a nature or degree that warrants detention in hospital. However, the consultant (RMO) Dr Lahmar states that she is a risk to her own health and safety. When cross examined on this point, Dr Lahmar states she is a risk to her own health or safety because she has a broken leg which needs time to heal. He states that this is why it is necessary to keep her in hospital as she is unwilling to wait to see a physiotherapist and he fears that she may cause her leg more damage if she is discharged before an assessment is arranged.

Sarah is discharged as the Tribunal are satisfied that she meets the discharge criteria. Although she is suffering from a mental illness, it is not of a nature or a degree to detain her in hospital. They make it clear that her broken leg is not a mental illness or disorder and consequently, as she has capacity, she cannot be detained to wait for a physiotherapy assessment even though staff may consider this to be in her best interests.

Case study 3: Nurse's holding power

Irene is a voluntary (informal) patient. However, staff have become increasingly concerned about her mental health and by the fact that Irene has been stating that she wishes to leave the ward.

Tracy, a ward nurse, is leaving the ward when before she is able to close the door behind her, Irene manages to push her way out.

Tracy is a nurse qualified to the Nursing and Midwifery Council level of registered nurse and decides that the circumstances necessitate her using her holding power under Section 5(4) to stop Irene and return her to the ward. She realises that there is not enough time to secure the attendance of a doctor to complete a Section 5(2) instead. After Tracy has secured Irene, she immediately bleeps Dr Sagoo. Mindful of the advice given in the Code of Practice, Dr Sagoo ensures she arrives on the ward as soon as possible and certainly no later than six hours after the Section 5(4) was initiated. On arrival, Dr Sagoo assesses Irene and applies Section 5(2) instead.

Case study 4: Interaction with the Mental Capacity Act

Jim is a voluntary (informal) patient on the older person's mental health ward. He lacks capacity in relation to his finances. Following assessment the junior doctor tells him that he needs a hip replacement. Jim is very upset by this news and is adamant that he does not want a hip replacement. Even when he is told about the serious consequences on his mobility should he not have one, he refuses to change his mind.

The junior doctor says that as Jim is on a mental health ward, she and another doctor and an approved social worker could detain him under the Mental Health Act so that he could then be forced to have the treatment. However the consultant, Dr Lahmar, points out the following to the junior doctor:

- ✓ Even if Jim was detained, it would not be possible to treat him under the Act as the hip replacement is not treatment for mental disorder.
- ✓ Jim does not have capacity in relation to his finances however, capacity is 'issue specific', so they need to assess Jim's capacity in relation to his decision not to have a hip replacement.
- ✓ Although the Mental Health Act cannot be used, if Jim is found to lack capacity in relation to this issue, common law powers may be used to make a best interests decision on Jim's behalf to have the hip replacement.
- ✓ After April 2007, the Mental Capacity Act 2005 should be used in place of common law powers in order to make an assessment of Jim's capacity and if appropriate then make a best interest's decision on his behalf.

Case study 5: Guardianship

Ingrid has been placed under guardianship by two doctors (one Section 12 approved) and an approved social worker. Under the guardianship powers, she has been told the following:

- ➢ She should reside at her mother's home.
- ➢ She should attend appointments with her GP every two weeks.
- ➢ She should take her medication (for mental illness)

Working With The Mental Health Act 1983

After a few weeks, her GP reports that Ingrid has missed an appointment and her mother reports that she does not reside at home every night and often goes without her medication.

The community mental health team discuss the case and a trainee social worker, Cassie, states that it is easily resolved as they can simply physically force her to attend the GP appointments, take her medication and reside at her mother's home.

She is quickly corrected by her supervisor Aziza who explains the following:

- ✓ Under the powers of guardianship, Ingrid can only be *required* to attend her GP appointments, reside at home and take her medication, she cannot be forced to do so.
- ✓ However, as it is vital for Ingrid's mental health that she take her medication, Aziza states that an approved social worker could apply for Ingrid to be assessed with a view to detaining her in hospital under Section 3 of the Act so that she may be forced to take her medication.

Case study 6: Removal to hospital of prisoners

Mark has been sent to prison recently on remand from the Magistrates' Court following a charge of theft. After a few days one of the prison officers, Chris, has become concerned because Mark has started talking to himself. Mark now complains to Chris that he cannot sleep at night because of voices in his head. Mark further explains that he is trying to resist the voices' instructions but is concerned he will not be able to do so for much longer.

Chris tells his supervisor who organises Mark's assessment by two doctors. Following assessment, it is agreed that Mark is suffering from *mental illness of a nature or degree which warrants detention and treatment in hospital and that this treatment is urgent.*

The Home Office is contacted, and having considered the doctors' recommendations, issue a transfer direction under Section 48 to move Mark from prison to hospital.

REFERENCES

1. The Information Centre, Mental Health Statistics Bulletin 2006/09/HSCIC (2006) *In-patients formally detained in hospitals under the Mental Health Act 1983 and other legislation, England 1994-95 to 2004-05.*

2. Commission for Healthcare Audit and Inspection (2005) *Count Me In, Results of a national census of in-patients in mental health hospitals and facilities in England and Wales, November 2005.*

3. Secretary of State for Health (1999) *Reform of the Mental Health Act 1983, proposals for consultation.*

4. Department of Health (2005) *Delivering race equality in mental health care: an action plan for reform inside and outside services.*

5. Information Centre for Health and Social Care (2005) *Guardianship under the Mental Health Act 1983: England 2005.*

6. The Home Office, Statistical Bulletin (2005) *Statistics of Mentally Disordered Offenders 2004.*

7. The Home Office (2006) *Notes for the guidance of supervising psychiatrists, Mental Health Act 1983, supervision and aftercare of conditionally discharged restricted patients.*

8. Department of Health (2006) *The Mental Health Bill: Plans to amend the Mental Health Act 1983, Briefing Sheets A1, A2, A3, A4, A5, A6, A7, A8.*

9. Mental Health Review Tribunal (2005) *Review of Activity, April 2001 to March 2005.*

10. Department of Health and the Welsh Office (1999) *Mental Health Act 1983, Code of Practice* ISBN 0-11-322111-8.

11. Department of Health and the Welsh Office (1998) *Mental Health Act 1983, Memorandum on Parts I to VI, VIII and X,* ISBN 0-11-322112-6.

12. Mental Health Act Commission (2004) *Safeguarding children and adolescents detained under the Mental Health Act 1983 on adult psychiatric ward.*

Further Reading

Richard Jones (2006) *Mental Health Act Manual, 10th Edition,* ISBN 0-421-96300-X

Mental Health Act - Statutory Forms		
Form	**Use**	**Section**
1	Application by nearest relative	Section 2
2	Application by approved social worker	Section 2
3	Medical recommendation - joint	Section 2
4	Medical recommendation - single	Section 2
5	Application by nearest relative	Section 4
6	Application by approved social worker	Section 4
7	Medical recommendation	Section 4
8	Application by nearest relative	Section 3
9	Application by approved social worker	Section 3
10	Medical recommendation - joint	Section 3
11	Medical recommendation - single	Section 3
12	Medical recommendation	Section 5(2)
13	Nursing recommendation (start of section)	Section 5(4)
14	Record of receipt of completed section papers	Section 2, 3, 4 & 5(2)
15	Record of receipt of medical recommendations	As applicable
16	Nursing report (end of section)	Section 5(4)
17	Guardianship - application by nearest relative	Section 7
18	Guardianship - application by approved social worker	Section 7
19	Guardianship – joint medical recommendation	Section 7
20	Guardianship – single medical recommendation	Section 7
21	Guardianship - acceptance of guardianship application	Section 7
22	Reclassification of detained patient	Section 16
23	Reclassification of patient under Guardianship	Section 16
24	Transfer - from one hospital (NHS Trust) to another	Section 19
25	Transfer - from hospital to guardianship	Section 19
26	Transfer - of patient to a new guardian	Section 19
27	Transfer - from guardianship to hospital	Section 19
28	Transfer - from guardianship to hospital joint medical form	Section 19
29	Transfer - from guardianship to hospital medical form	Section 19
30	Renewal (extension) of detention	Section 20
31	Renewal (extension) of guardianship	Section 20
31A	AWOL – return after more than 28 days AWOL detained	Section 21

Working With The Mental Health Act 1983

31B	AWOL – return after more than 28 days AWOL guardianship	Section 21
32	Classification of patient	Section 92
33	Reception of a patient removed to England and Wales	Part VI
34	Nearest relative – discharge from hospital request	Section 23
35	Nearest relative - discharge from guardianship request	Section 23
36	Nearest relative - barring of discharge by RMO	Section 25
37	Treatment – certificate of consent and second opinion	Section 57
38	Treatment – certificate of consent	Section 58
39	Treatment – certificate of second opinion	Section 58
1S	Supervised discharge – application	Section 25
2S	Supervised discharge – medical recommendation	Section 25
3S	Supervised discharge – approved social worker's form	Section 25
4S	Supervised discharge – reclassification of disorder	Section 25
5S	Supervised discharge - renewal	Section 25
6S	Supervised discharge - discharge	Section 25

Patient Rights Leaflets
(available from *www.markwalton.net*)

Leaflet	Title	Section
1	Nurse's holding power	Section 5(4)
2	Admission for assessment in cases of emergency	Section 4
3	Application in respect of patient already in hospital	Section 5(2)
4	Warrant to search and remove	Section 135(1)
5	Police power of arrest	Section 136
6	Admission for assessment	Section 2
7	Admission for treatment	Section 3
8	Hospital order	Section 37
9	Hospital order with restrictions	Section 37/41
10	Guardianship order	Section 7
11	Court appointed guardianship order	Section 37
12	Court hospital order and restricted hospital order	Sections 37 and 37/41
13	Patients' letters	Section 134
14	Remand to hospital for assessment	Section 35
15	Remand to hospital for treatment	Section 36
16	Interim hospital order	Section 38
17	Supervised discharge	Section 25
18	Transfer from prison with restrictions	Section 47/49
19	Transfer from prison	Section 47
20	Transfer from prison	Sections 48 and 48/49
21	Information for nearest relatives	All

Mental Health Act Commission – Information Leaflets (available from *www.mhac.org.uk*)		
Leaflet	**1**	Information about the Mental Health Act Commission
	2	Information about consent to treatment (medication)
	3	Information about consent to electroconvulsive therapy (ECT)
	4	Information about how to make a complaint
	5	Information about neurosurgery for mental disorder (psychosurgery)

Mental Health Act Commission – Guidance Notes (available from *www.mhac.org.uk*)	
Subject	**Title**
Code	Status of the Code of Practice following the House of Lords' Munjaz ruling
Code	Suggested annotations to reflect case law and other changes – issue 2
Seclusion	Guidance for commissioners on monitoring the use of seclusion
Voting	Voting and detained patient guidance note
Minors	Children and adolescents admitted formally under the Act on adult wards
Anorexia	Guidance on the treatment of anorexia nervosa
Clozapine	Guidance on the administration of clozapine and other treatments
Hospitals	Use of the Act in general hospitals without a psychiatric unit
GPs	General practitioners and the Act
Private care	Issues relating to the administration of the Act in independent hospitals
Leave/Transfer	Issues surrounding Sections 17, 18 and 19 of the Act
Nurses	Nurses, the administration of medication for mental disorder and the Act
RMOs	Guidance for RMOs following the PS case
RMOs	Guidance for RMOs: R v Dr Feggetter and the MHAC
SOADs	People with nursing qualifications and consultation with the other professional in second opinions under the Act
SOADs	Guidance for SOADs: R v Dr Feggetter and the MHAC
Forms	Scrutinising and rectifying forms for admission under the Act
Consent	Consent guidance for commissioners
Relative	Nearest relatives of non-UK residents
Relative	Guidance on the rights of nearest relative under the Act

Part 1		**Application of the Act**
Section	1	Definition of mental disorders
Part II		**Compulsory admission to hospital and guardianship**
Section	2	Admission for assessment
	3	Admission for treatment
	4	Emergency admission for assessment
	5	Application for a patient already in hospital
	6	Effect of application for admission
	7	Application for guardianship
	8	Effect of guardianship
	9	Regulations as to guardianship
	10	Transfer of guardianship in case of death, incapacity, etc of guardian
	11	General provisions as to applications
	12	General provisions as to medical recommendations
	13	Duty of approved social workers to make applications
	14	Social reports
	15	Errors on forms and their rectification
	16	Reclassification of mental disorder
	17	Leave of absence from hospital
	18	Return and readmission of patients absent without leave
	19	Transfer of patients
	20	Duration of detention
	21	Special provisions as to patients absent without leave
	21A	Patients taken into custody or returned within 28 days
	21B	Patients taken into custody or returned after more than 28 days
	22	Special provisions for patients sentenced to imprisonment etc
	23	Discharge of patients
	24	Visiting and examination of patients
	25	Restrictions on discharge by nearest relative
	25A	Supervised discharge – application
	25B	Supervised discharge – making of applications
	25C	Supervised discharge – supplementary applications
	25D	Supervised discharge – after-care requirements
	25E	Supervised discharge – review of after-care
	25F	Supervised discharge – reclassification of mental disorder
	25G	Supervised discharge – duration and renewal
	25H	Supervised discharge – discharge
	25I	Supervised discharge – provisions for those sentenced or imprisoned
	25J	Supervised discharge – transfer from Scotland to England and Wales
	26	Definition of 'relative' and 'nearest relative'
	27	Children and young persons in care
	28	Nearest relative of minor under guardianship etc
	29	Appointment by Court of acting nearest relative
	30	Discharge and variation of orders under Section 29
	31	Applications to the County Court
	32	Regulations that can be made with regard to the Act
	33	Special provisions as to wards of Court
	34	Definitions – responsible medical officer etc

Part VI	**Removal and return of patients within United Kingdom etc**	
Section	80	Removal of patients to Scotland
	81	Removal of patients to Northern Ireland
	82	Removal to England and Wales of patients from Northern Ireland
	83	Removal of patients to Channel Islands or Isle of Man
	84	Removal to England and Wales of offenders found insane in Channel Islands and Isle of Man
	85	Patients removed from Channel Islands or Isle of Man
	86	Removal of alien patients
	87	Patients absent from hospitals in Northern Ireland
	88	Patients absent from hospitals in England and Wales
	89	Patients absent from hospitals in Channel Islands or Isle of Man
	90	Regulations for Part VI
	91	General provisions as to patients removed from England and Wales
	92	Interpretation of Part VI
Part VII	**Management of Property and Affairs**	
		This part of the Act will be completely rescinded with the introduction of the Mental Capacity Act 2005 in April 2007.
Part VIII	**Miscellaneous**	
Section	114	Appointment of approved social workers
	115	Power of entry and inspection by social workers
	116	Duty of local authority to visit certain patients
	117	Duty to provide after-care
	118	Code of practice
	119	Payment of medical practitioners under Part IV
	120	General protection of detained patients
	121	Mental Health Act Commission
	122	Provision of pocket money for in-patients in hospital
	123	Transfers to and from special hospitals
	124	Default powers of the Secretary of State
	125	Inquiries
Part IX	**Offences**	
Section	126	Forgery, false statements etc
	127	Ill-treatment of patients
	128	Assisting patients to absent themselves without leave etc
	129	Obstruction
	130	Prosecutions by local authorities
Part X	**Miscellaneous and supplementary**	
Section	131	Informal admission of patients
	132	Duty of hospitals to give information to detained patients
	133	Duty of hospitals to inform nearest relative of discharge
	134	Correspondence of patients
	135	Warrant to search for and remove patients
	136	Police power of arrest
	137	Provisions as to custody, conveyance and detention
	138	Retaking of patients escaping from custody
	139	Protection for acts done in pursuance of the Act
	140	Reception of urgent cases

Working With The Mental Health Act 1983

These questions are all related to topics covered within this guide and will allow you to test your knowledge of the Act.

Q: What is the maximum period of detention allowed under Section 2?
A: 28 days.

Q: What is the maximum period of detention allowed under Section 3?
A: Six months. Unless it is extended (renewed).

Q: Who must be involved in order to detain someone under Section 2 or 3?
A: Two doctors (one of whom should be Section 12 approved) and an approved social worker or the nearest relative.

Q: Which section gives the shortest holding power under the Act and what is the maximum time for which it can be used?
A: Section 5(4), lasts six hours.

Q: What is required to give electro-convulsive therapy (ECT) to a detained patient?
A: The patient's consent or a second opinion doctor's agreement.

Q: Name three sections which can bring someone from the community into hospital?
A: Sections 2, 3, 4, 135(1), 135(2) and 136.

Q: Which part of the Act deals with forensic (Court and prison) sections?
A: Part III.

Q: Which forensic sections of the Act allow Courts to sentence a person to hospital for treatment?
A: Sections 37 and 37/41.

Q: Which sections of the Act allow forcible entry to premises to look for and remove a person?
A: Sections 135(1) and 135(2).

Q: Who issues the warrant under Sections 135(1) and 135(2)?
A: A magistrate.

Q: Over which section of the Act do police have sole jurisdiction?
A: Section 136.

Q: What does Section 136 allow the police to do?
A: Move a person who fits the legal criteria for Section 136 from a public place to a place of safety for assessment.

Q: Name two sections which can only be used in the community?
A: Section 7 guardianship order and Section 25 supervised discharge.

Q: Can a person under a Section 7 guardianship order be treated without their consent?
A: No.

Q: Which requirements can be placed upon someone under a Section 7 guardianship order?

A: *Requirement to reside at a particular address, attend appointments and give access to doctors, approved social workers or other staff.*

Q: How do guardianship and supervised discharge differ compared with the rest of the Act?

A: *Age limit. The above two sections have a minimum age limit of 16 whereas the rest of the Act does not set a minimum age limit.*

Q: Put these people in the correct order in terms of the hierarchy of nearest relatives: Sister (age 38), nephew, brother (age 34), mother.

A: *Mother, sister, brother, nephew.*

Q: Which staff can grant leave of absence for people detained under Section 2 or 3?

A: *Only the consultant (RMO) or, in their absence, the doctor in charge of their treatment.*

Q: For people detained under forensic restricted sections who can grant leave?

A: *The consultant (RMO) can request leave but only the Home Office can grant it.*

Q: Name two forms of Mental Health Act hearings.

A: *Hospital Managers' hearings and Mental Health Review Tribunals.*

Q: Who normally appears to give evidence at a Mental Health Act hearing?

A: *A consultant (RMO), an approved social worker, a ward nurse and the patient.*

Q: Can a voluntary (informal) patient who has capacity to consent be forced to accept treatment under the Act?

A: *No. Only patients detained under certain sections of the Act can be forcibly treated.*

Q: Which section of the Act places a duty upon health and social services to provide after-care to patients detained under the Act?

A: *Section 117.*

Q: Does the Act allow post being sent by a detained person to be withheld?

A: *Yes.*

Q: Is a person detained under the Act allowed to vote?

A: *Yes, although forensic (Court and prison) sections are excluded.*

Q: Which Act must also be considered when dealing with children?

A: *The Children Act 1989.*

Q: Name three methods of dealing with the finances of someone who lacks capacity.

A: *Enduring powers of attorney (soon to be lasting powers of attorney), receivership (soon to become deputies) and appointeeship.*

Q: Where in the UK does the Act apply?

A: *England and Wales.*

Q: Does the Code of Practice have the same authority in law as the Act?

A: *No.*

Mental Disorder

Mental disorder as used in the Act means mental illness, arrested or incomplete development of mind (mental impairment), psychopathic disorder and any other disorder or disability of mind. The legislation gives definitions for three of the specific disorders required by many of the detaining sections but leaves mental illness to be defined by clinical staff.

Severe Mental Impairment

A state of arrested or incomplete development of mind (learning disability) which includes severe impairment of intelligence and social functioning and is associated with abnormally aggressive or seriously irresponsible conduct on the part of the person concerned.

Mental Impairment

A state of arrested or incomplete development of mind (not amounting to severe mental impairment) which includes significant impairment of intelligence and social functioning and is associated with abnormally aggressive and or seriously irresponsible conduct on the part of the person concerned.

Psychopathic Disorder

A persistent disorder or disability of the mind whether or not including significant impairment of intelligence which results in abnormally aggressive or seriously irresponsible conduct on the part of the person concerned.

Exclusions from the definition of Mental Disorder

The following are specifically excluded from the definition of mental disorder:

- ➢ Immoral conduct
- ➢ Promiscuity
- ➢ Sexual deviance
- ➢ Alcohol dependency
- ➢ Drug addiction

Although the above may be linked to or may be symptoms of mental illness they are not in themselves enough to allow detention.

*   *   *   *   *

Approved Social Worker (ASW)

A social worker with additional training on the Act who is then approved by a local authority to carry out specific duties under the legislation.

Nearest Relative

See page 92.

Responsible Medical Officer (RMO)

The doctor in charge of the treatment of the patient (consultant psychiatrist) or if a person is subject to guardianship, the doctor authorised by the local social services authority to act as the responsible medical officer. The role has specific legal duties and powers attached to it.

Second Opinion Approved Doctor (SOAD)

A doctor approved by the Mental Health Act Commission to give second opinions as required under the consent to treatment procedures contained in the Act.